CLAQ

Creating Love & Asking Questions

Martin "Mark" Tomback

MOORING
FIELD
BOOKS

CLAQ

Creating Love & Asking Questions
Martin "Mark" Tomback

Published by:

MOORING FIELD BOOKS

Mooring Field Books
10354 Fairway Road
Pembroke Pines, FL 33026
(954) 629-8078
mooringfieldbooks@msn.com
www.claqonline.com

First Printing 2015
Cover Design by Martin Tomback
Printed In the United States of America
Disclaimer: This book is intended to provide accurate information with regard to the subject matter covered. However, the author and publisher accept no responsibility for inaccuracies or omissions and the author and publisher specifically disclaim any liability, loss or risk, personal, financial, or otherwise, which is incurred as a consequence, directly or indirectly, from the use and/or application of any of the contents of this book.

Publisher's Cataloging–in-Publication
Tomback, Martin.
CLAQ : creating love & asking questions/
by Martin "Mark" Tomback.
p. cm.
LCCN 2015904287
ISBN 978-0-9755248-2-4
1. Psychology, Religious. 2. Spiritual life. 3. Self-actualization (Psychology)–Self-improvement. 4. Well-being—Religious aspects. 5. Spiritual-mindedness. I. Title.
BL51-65 2015 200

Dedication

This book is dedicated to Gloria, Mirabelle, and Pearl

For their eternal love and support.

Yes, your "Never-never country"—
yes, your "edge of cultivation"
And "no sense in going further"—
till I crossed the range to see.
God forgive me! No, I didn't.
It's God's present to our nation.
Anybody might have found it,
but—His Whisper came to Me!

The Explorer (1898)
by Rudyard Kipling

Table of Contents

The Author

I'm a mystic. It's not something I planned on being. Someone told me I was a mystic. It sounded exotic and powerful, like Dr. Strange in the old Marvel comics with lightning bolts shooting from his hands. I always knew I was different so it made sense. Even as a boy I was interested in the nature of my existence. I often had moments of conscious self-awareness so it fit. I was very impressed with myself when I had the thought, "What the hell is a mystic?" It was a year before it came to me. It just popped into my head. I always figured an angel whispered it to me. A mystic is someone with no separation from God. So for all you mystics out there, here's something to think about.

It doesn't make me better than anyone else. It makes me more capable in certain areas. It's the same as a strong person having an advantage in sports or an assertive, personable person excelling in business. It's a God-given talent, like having a beautiful voice. It's satisfying and it's a responsibility. It's fun to be close to God's love, to know God as a friend in a conversational way. It's comforting to feel God's support. But it's not something I have that no one else has. Everyone has it. With attention and practice it can be improved in the same way training helps an athlete or advertising helps the businessperson. Anyone can strengthen the link between themselves and God. But I don't have to make an effort to have that conscious contact. It's like I'm always there in constant prayer.

So here's a story I amuse myself with to describe my purpose. It starts in Heaven. I'm sitting on a cloud, minding my own business, when two angels walk up. They say God wants to see me. It has the feel of the movie *Apocalypse Now* where the military police come for the young captain at his hotel in Saigon. My first thought is, "Jeez, what did I do wrong?" Then I think, "Well, I haven't seen God in a while and it's always fun so this should be good." We leave and head for the Hall of Paradise where God holds court. It's a massive Greek temple-like building in perfect condition. At the entrance there's an angel waiting for me, a small one about four feet tall. The angel says, "I'm so glad you're here. God wants to see you." The hall is filled with everyone seeking God's favor. So we walk up along the side. There's a walkway separated from the main room by a series of columns. Now, everyone's eyes are on God with the exception of a small group in the back. They don't have any interest in what's going on. Some are sitting, some standing. They're just talking among themselves...until I walk in. Then the whole group stops, turns to the door, and locks their eyes on me. It's a tough-looking bunch; ten foot tall Archangels, Norse Gods, not the cherubic types. I break eye contact and follow the angel up front. Then I shoot a glance over my shoulder and they're still looking at me, following me with their eyes.

We get up front where my escort tells me to wait while he pushes his way through the crowd. Then he reaches out and tugs on God's robe for attention. God leans forward and the angel says I've arrived. God looks up. With a big smile, God asks me to sit down. "I'm glad you've come. Let me finish here. I want to talk to you." So God finishes and asks the hall to be cleared. In an instant it's empty...with one exception. The group at the back, the group staring at me, they're still there, but now they're staring at me and God. "How are you, Mark?" "Fine." I say. God's happy to hear it. "Great. Anything you need?" "No. Thanks, Boss." Again, God smiles and says, "Fine." Then God leans forward and says, "Mark, I'd like you to do me a favor. I'd like you to go to Earth and make life easier for people." A favor, I told you it's fun getting together with God. "Sure. I'm happy to help. Whatever you need." Then God says, "I don't want you to worry." So I think, "Worried about doing a favor for God, I'm not worried." Then God goes, "I don't want you to worry so I'm sending you some help." and motions to the group in the back. Now, I'm worried. I think, "What on Earth am I getting into if this is the juice

I'm going to need." But, I say, "Thanks, Boss. I'll be okay. I'd like to do it myself." "It could get rough, Mark. I think you should take the help." "No. I can do it." I insist. Then, God, with a sullen face and a few short nods, says, "Okay. Call me if you need me." So I come to Earth. But as soon as I leave, God beckons the group from the back and says, "Follow him down. He's got a good heart and he's reliable, not always sensible, but an honest heart. Make sure he doesn't get into trouble." Well, that's who I think I am and that's why I think I'm here.

Introduction

Control. That's what this is about, your ability to accept responsibility and control your life. It starts with your desire to change things, then you decide what you want, and do what you need to achieve it. It's simple but it isn't easy. Desire is easy. You feel it before you can define it. Your challenge is to make it happen and have the patience to be comfortable with the process. There are actions to take, steps to achieve, evaluations to make, and constant planning. Then, your accomplishment happens. It's not a never-ending road. Growth is your goal. Your problems get resolved. You master yourself and finally reach the happiness you seek. Then there comes a time when you advance beyond your lessons. Problems come and go but your maturity becomes your being.

Mastery is your influence. It's how you affect the changes in your life. It doesn't mean eliminating your problems, though it often starts there. Life is knowing your nature, having goals, and developing your talents so they satisfy your dignity. Being a master is like a sea captain whose responsibility is to know everything about their ship. You have to understand how you control your ship. You want to do it without punishing yourself to perform but instead knowing your abilities and applying them even when your best choice is to seek help. Different tasks need different skills. A master knows their limits and projects their influence, not their ability. Like a dependable ship, you are your ability. Whether your ship is a cruise liner or an oil tanker, it's adaptable. It's not limited by its design. As a master, you look for the opportunities in change, see the limits, and know when something new is needed.

A master doesn't wave a wand to fix a problem. They engage it. It's in realizing your talents and using your support. In this way, you guide yourself along life's currents. Nature has its purpose and you have your purpose. But you also have free will. You have the freedom to create your satisfaction.

Your world isn't stable for long, even when you want it to be. You'd like to sit back and enjoy your accomplishments, like the juggler who finally gets all the plates spinning on their sticks. But, inevitably, some slow down, wobble, and the juggler has to race forward to attend them and keep them spinning. Yet, in this hectic act of juggling, they keep adding plates to show they can do more and still be successful. They want you to admire their accomplishment. They hope the audience understands the difficulty, laughs when it becomes too much for them, and applauds their success. No one cares if you can spin dinner plates on a stick. Its purpose is entertainment. There's no meaning other than the mastery to achieve it. It's the mastery that awes you. It's the mastery you want.

Everything is growing, even when you're not watching it. Your life and universal consciousness grow. So how do you control it? How do you know who you are so you can create the growth you want?

There's stability in life that you might overlook. The mechanical part is easy. You don't tinker with it because it's a structure you trust. It's the stage where you perform, like the juggler, a solid base for getting in front of the crowd. The scenery may change but you understand it. It doesn't need your attention. The question is if it's the stage where you want to perform. A different venue may suit you better. It may mean moving out of your comfort zone and deciding if your old habits still serve you.

You mature. Maturity means you grow ethically, respecting your responsibilities. It means improving your ability to help yourself, having positive relationships, and recognizing that you have a relationship with God. Your maturity is psychological, including your education, and emotional, including the courage your life demands. The things you want have conflicting values. You have to understand them to make good choices. You have to control your emotions so your choices are guided by common sense, not the dread of a possible failure. It doesn't matter where you are. It's up to you to choose if there's someplace you'd rather be, and do what you need to get there.

You react to your circumstances. Problems are distractions. Whether they're real or imagined doesn't matter. The effect is real and must be resolved to move you forward in the least restrictive way. Every change you trust is a step to trust yourself more. You feel control when you're honest with yourself. Focus the features of your feelings into the picture of where you want to be. Your challenge is to reduce the influence of your problems and get your mind working on the means to create your happiness.

Changing your life is usually an easy choice even when it means committing to a new idea. Once you make a change, it's done. You move forward. The beauty is how your courage builds your confidence. Mastery is your accumulation of confidence. Perfect choices are rare and unnecessary. You have plenty to work with where you are. Change is a challenge because you have to compare the cost and benefit of unknown circumstances. You may only get one chance, or your choice may mean years of commitment with no guarantee of success. And it may be hard to redo it if you didn't make the right choice. Some changes are simple, like choosing your clothes in the morning. Others take courage because they mean reforming your life. Your choice for change probably won't be comfortable, but you're probably not comfortable now. Opportunities present themselves and you build on them. Your desire for change doesn't just happen. It develops. You decide when you commit yourself completely.

So what about life can you change? Firstly, your name, you can change your legal or social identity. You can change it to Mommy, Boss, or whatever you like. You can ask people to call you by your first name or with the prefix Mr., Mrs., or Ms. It can be a socially acceptable nickname like "Lucky" or "Chuck" or a unique email address that describes something about you. It represents an identity other than your birth name. Changing your name changes your identity into something that suits your opinion of yourself. You can do it for whatever reason you like. I changed my name from Martin to Mark. My legal papers are in my given name but for the past twenty years everybody calls me Mark. It's confusing to old friends but it resonates with me. It's a common reason people change their names and you can do it whenever you like.

"Mark" suits me. It was a shock for my mother but she came around. It was still me. Try to feel how your name touches your identity. Take someone's business card and use it to introduce yourself. It's an odd feeling taking someone else's name. It matters, and then again, it doesn't. So pick a name that makes you feel good. It's normal to use nicknames like "Princess" or "Big Jim" or make up anything you like. It's easy for meeting new people. There's no history to explain. You're the person you introduce yourself to be.

Change your appearance. Get a new hairstyle. Dress to express your values. Go high fashion or live in shorts and a t-shirt. Tell the world who you are. Make yourself known to those who think the same way you do. It's easy to jumpstart a change because it makes you feel good right away. Find the courage to be who you are. Look like you belong.

Change where you live. Reorient yourself. Fresh surroundings make everything new; the people you see, the roads you drive, the stores you use. It doesn't matter if it's across town or the other side of the world. It's an adventure. Choose it. Change your furniture. It could be a new couch or a widescreen TV. Watching TV is a big part of people's lives. That alone can spark good feelings. You begin to feel comfortable in your new space. Everything you encounter is a world you created.

Change your car. You spend so much time in it, it's part of you. The car you *choose* expresses who you are. It goes beyond appearances because it states what you want it to do: go fast, be luxurious, be flashy, or just plain transportation. It's the icon of the mid-life crisis when someone buys a sports car to hold onto their youth. Why not do it now and be the person you want to be? Control your changes. Maybe you don't look the part yet, but if you drive a car that says who you are you can let your hair grow into it.

You control your changes as much as you can. You decide your priorities. It's harder when your decisions affect others. You don't have the freedom simply to satisfy yourself. You have responsibilities to your relationships. If you're married, you can get divorced and start fresh. If you're single, you can marry and join a partner for new opportunities. But what about your children? What about your relations? What about your friends? You have to review everything to see what changed and why you're looking for new opportunities. Relationships are agreements. They require respect in the same way you respect yourself. Changing them requires new agreements. A change can be emotional and hard to accept. Breaking emotional bonds is no simple adjustment when others are involved.

Change involves money. That's always a test. If you have a business, it's not easy to walk away. Business relationships are built on dependability. Change concerns customers who rely on the stability of your business. If you have a job, can you find something better that pays you what you need? You still have to survive. Change is the time for courage. If you're not working, find a job that makes you feel good. If you like what you're doing, ask for a promotion, new tasks, or a different workplace. Move to a new company. Start a new career. Enjoy the energy where life excites you. New relationships can help you break the habits you've outgrown. It isn't easy. It's important. So much revolves around your work that it's the perfect place for changes in your life. Use it to trigger the changes you choose.

Mastery is learned. Then you can enjoy the qualities that make your life unique. I changed my life. I got divorced and lost my job at the same time. It was scary but I was free. It doesn't matter how it happened. It understands that controlling a change is possible. Change creates opportunities, or you could say forces opportunities on you. Even when you think your life is stable, every day takes courage and effort as the vicissitudes of life bounce you around. I was a person who accommodated so much of life's pressure that I lost myself. A lost person is unhappy. Your changes may not solve your problems. You choose a path for its benefits then try to hold onto whatever goodness you sacrificed for it. Respect the risks but be free. Freedom controls your responsibilities. Freedom is your happiness. Your mastery will teach it to you.

Chapter 1
A New Life

Bullying (Why bully me? I was such a nice kid.)

I had a blissful childhood till I was about eight years old. My family didn't have a lot of money then, but I didn't know it. I didn't even know it mattered. There were always opportunities. My dad worked hard and did well over the years but I'll never forget the year I got shoe trees and sweat socks for Christmas. Any toy would have been fine, but that morning's joyful anticipation became a crushing disappointment when I received the worst gift a child could imagine...shoe trees. Though we didn't have a lot of money, growing up in East Meadow, Long Island was always safe and clean. Until I was eight years old my brother had no interest in me. He's about five and a half years older and I adored him. But at eight I began to shine. I was placed in an advanced placement class in elementary school and I skipped a grade. I started getting more attention from my parents. That's when my brother's jealousy showed up and the bullying began.

I was at a disadvantage because I still adored him and wanted him to like me, but it became endless teasing that turned me into his servant and an emotional punching bag. To my detriment I accepted it. I tried to please him but the bullying didn't stop. For protection I withdrew into myself and became terribly frightened of people not liking me. I didn't get a lot of approval in those days. My dad was always working or with his friends. My mom had the simple interests

1

of a 1950s housewife. And my brother was plain mean. So I stopped expressing myself because I always expected to be rejected. That's what I had become accustomed to.

It was horrible training for life. It was all in my head and took me decades to heal. Many years of small successes then, after the death of my mother, a deep understanding of the negative habits I had formed dealing with my brother. Those habits followed me into adulthood. My brother had looted my mom's estate and I felt terrible I had let it happen. It took me seven years to get over it. I was in my late fifties. Those habits had bound me my whole life like chains. Inside I was still a nice kid but I suffered the conflict of not treating myself fairly. I refused to accept it. That conflict led me to the deep introspection that introduced me to the powerful parts of myself I enjoy today. It takes time but it's doable. And I had some advantages. I'm smart and God's a friend of mine.

The Attitude for Change

A new life is the same for everyone. For the teenager entering a world they barely know, regardless of their bravado, the world expects them to be responsible. The retiree enters a new way of life without the resources they're accustomed to, including their health and finances. For the divorced person, now alone, life's uncertainties present frightening choices burdened by the responsibilities of their previous marriage. The ex-convict or recovering addict encounters the stigma of their history on top of life's normal unpredictability. Anytime you want to change, you need to master the nature of your human condition.

Every day you start a new life. You wake up and everything's fresh. Yesterday's responsibilities are still with you, but opportunity has returned. When you release the emotions attached to yesterday's problems you can regain the objectivity that lets you approach them from a new perspective. Creative solutions are your goal because you can never guarantee your influence in a situation. All you can do is improve your control to create an environment that promotes what you want.

A creative solution should be simple. It should lead you to connections you hadn't seen before. Your responsibilities can distract you from simple solutions. Life forces you to deal with problems when they come up, not when it's convenient. This guides you to create routines that support you without much attention. Routines provide the unconscious support that relieves your mind of its basic tasks so you can use all your creativity.

It's important to control your routines. A routine shouldn't make you a robot. Taking the same way to work when you know the road is blocked is foolish. A routine is a tool. Be ready to change it when you can improve it. Monitor your routines to keep them effective. See your routines as an extension of your home, a safe place to catch your breath and make new plans.

A change starts where you are and *through your desire* arrives somewhere new. So feel your dreams. Your control is your sensitivity to your circumstances so your first job is to pay attention. What you don't understand, learn. What you can't do, practice. What you don't like, remove, whether it's quitting a boring job or leaving old friends who hold you back. Teach yourself who you are. Life is simple. Either you like something or you don't. Change is complicated. The result could be anything. Your situation is the result of other situations and when circumstances change it can be hard to accommodate your current relationships and still respect yourself.

Use patience.

Evaluations take time but you can do it. You know the people in your life. You know your situations. Start with an overview with you at the center. This isn't being selfish. It's your responsibility to take care of yourself first. How you balance it with your respect for others is the trick. You must know that what you do affects everything. Some things you'll like. Other things you'll wonder how you ever let *that* happen. Social responsibilities connect you even when you don't want them. You learn to deal with what life gives you. The question is never, "Can you handle it?" You can always handle it. The question is, "How do you control the changes and be responsible when the best choice is that someone's going to get less?" Two people can't use the car at the same time. The answer to the question of fairness requires patience. What you can't have now, you can probably get later.

Patience uses fairness to balance its responsibilities. Patience is a skill. Your creativity wants its satisfaction *now* to move forward. Patience doesn't ignore your responsibilities. It's your realization that pieces of a problem can take time to transform to the point where your influence can affect them. Patience is your comfort with the process. When you can't pick someone up on time who's waiting for you for a ride, asking them to wait fifteen minutes is a fair alternative.

Patience is a feeling. You know what it is but how do you know you're successful at it? It's the comfort in knowing what's right for you. Life isn't always clear. And there's more than one way to do things. In maturing you learn that you do the right thing not when you wait but when you're patient.

Patience is part of control. It believes in your inevitable success. It's a comfortable place to consider your situation. Patience is the confidence that calms your emotions. There you can think through the issues without the pressure of time limits. Through patience you find alternatives. Patience respects your considerations so you know you did your best. Patience doesn't waste time. Like I did, you need courage to take the time to write a book with no guarantee anyone will read it. Patience gave me the courage. It's your free will because it's not directed by fear. It's supported by the belief that you'll eventually achieve your goal despite the difficulties. Patience believes in divine solutions and doing what you can while you wait for Creation to catch up.

Patience is a mature attitude. Most people believe speed and power solve problems. The physics make sense. Patience opens you to more opportunities. Patience doesn't ignore speed and power but employs them more effectively; how, when, and where to use them. It's a total approach using everything possible, including your spirituality. You're more effective when your body, mind, and spirit work together. Like the farmer who rotates their crops each year to avoid depleting the soil, patience respects the schedule everything needs to be most productive.

Patience supports you when you're up against an unexpected change. It could be the death of a family member or a business associate changing jobs. It could be something you've worked on for years finally reaching fruition. Life's twists and turns can undercut the dependability of what you've built or bless you with unexpected success. Plans change. It could be a problem or an opportunity. Regardless of the suddenness of a change, patience makes it manageable. It doesn't slow you down. It prioritizes the details so you can focus on the task at hand.

Patience trusts God's plan for you. If you don't believe in God then rely on the positive effects you see from being patient and disregard its meaning while you let your patience do its job. Patience is a fact. You help your roses grow by fertilizing them. Then you wait and let nature do its job. You don't snap your fingers and a rose appears. Things must be nourished in their own way to do their best. Patience is your choice to let things grow. Patience can be your faith when you believe you'll be successful no matter how long it takes.

How do you go from, "Patience sounds good. I want to be patient." to making patience your second nature? You start with a desire to change. Then you work at it till you have it. A goal takes time whether you're patient with it or not. You know what it's like waiting for service at a restaurant. You just don't want to worry about it. You want to be respected. You control your patience by using your time the best way you can. Adding time is the essence of patience. You may plan your patience to the minute but you have to give it whatever time it needs to give you what you want.

Patience takes practice. Like any skill, you teach it to yourself. The beauty is it becomes part of your character. Improving your character is the most productive thing you can do. Your character is the collection of personality tools you use to manage your life. Your character grows with the simple thought that you want to be a better person. You may want to build your confidence so you can give a better speech. Patience is the path to confidence. Patience is learnable. You develop it. You know what it is but incorporating it into your consciousness means trusting yourself and trusting life will cooperate. It's being aware of yourself when you're impatient and releasing it without punishing yourself.

Impatience is hell. It dreads what might happen if you don't get what you want right away. It prizes immediacy when speed doesn't matter, like racing your car to a red light then having to wait till the light turns green. It's rushing without a real need for urgency. It's your demand that life must be the fantasy you trust even when nature wants something else. Impatiently you demand relief, but it's your imagination not your reality. It's demanding completion even when completion isn't ready.

Nothing happens because you demand it. Life's ups and downs fine tune your maturity. Your perfection grows. Parts of you complete themselves and affect other parts that wait for their development so they can complete themselves and become part of the next process in line. Small steps refine who you are. Your life isn't about performing surgery with an ax even if it gets the job done. Impatience is crude and results in bad feelings and unnecessary problems. Accomplishments are a series of processes directed by you to serve your purpose. Patience is practical because it gives you better ways to use your time.

Enthusiasm: Controlling Your Passions

Change works with your emotions…your *enthusiasm*. You can feel it. You express it when you cheer for your team. You jump up and down. You yell as loud as you can to focus your emotions into a sledgehammer that empowers your team and disheartens the opponent. "Yea for us!" you shriek. But is that the limit of the power in your enthusiasm? Is excitement all it is or is it something finer, stronger, like steel is to iron? Is there a better way you can use your enthusiasm?

Enthusiasm is misunderstood when it's described as "ambition" or "rowdiness." That's not what it is. When you appreciate your enthusiasm its potential goes beyond your circumstances. Enthusiasm is your joy engaging life. Enthusiasm expresses itself in engagement, not accomplishment. It's your joy in life despite the challenges. It's your thrill in life's possibilities. Enthusiasm elevates your joy above your fear so you can always be confident. It's a ride on a roller coaster. "Let's do it again!" you gush. Like Oliver Hardy's famous line to his comedy partner Stan Laurel, "This is another fine mess you've gotten us into."

Enthusiasm is easily mistaken by its appearance. It's not persistence or perseverance. Those are goal-oriented attitudes. It's not energetic effort. That's its power, not its meaning. It's not your passion, though enthusiasm is often seen as suffering for your goal. Enthusiasm is more. Passion is the negative side of desire. It focuses on its hardships. Enthusiasm is the positive side of desire. Enthusiasm sees opportunities, not problems. Enthusiasm is about your actions, not their price. Problems are incidental to your enthusiasm. Enthusiasm raises your desire spiritually to where you enjoy the game and don't worry about the score. That's why amateur athletes work so hard when their reward for winning is a medal.

Enthusiasm doesn't accept something's okay because everyone's doing it. It's not a riot. Without love, life fails. Enthusiasm is an attitude, an internal belief about yourself. Life's process is one part. Your spiritual purpose is the other part. Life challenges you to choose which is more important at the moment. Your purpose brings your life and soul together to serve each other. Enthusiasm is your spiritual power released into life. It breathes God's love into everything you do. Your goals evolve, but your enthusiasm remains love's joy forever.

Joy: Something You Want That You Already Have

Joy sees the goodness in everything. Even though you work at it, it's easy to lose in your changing emotions. "Joy" is a strange word because it seems to lack power. It brings up images of babies and flowers because it's a spiritual word. Joy can be the sweet memory in grief or the divine acceptance in gallows humor. Spirituality always seems to lack the strength it deserves. Joy really means mastery. Joy approaches everything, favorable or not, as a puzzle. That's why video games are so popular. They mimic your desire to master your life. Joy is its finer sense. It's the fun beyond your satisfaction. It's the actual process of loving everything. Without love, nothing in life would interest you. Feeling love is joy.

Your joy controls everything. It wants the best for you. It's your awareness of opportunities. Where engagement is your goal, every problem has value. Joy doesn't fear your life. It respects it. Joy isn't your comfort. It creates it. It's the confidence a mountain climber feels when they see a view only meant for those who climb to the top.

Identify your joy. That's your goal, not what you attach to it. Joy completes you. Joy may seem beyond your ability, like when you want a loved one who's passed away to share in your current success. But, that's life. It doesn't diminish your joy. Your joy is complete when it accepts disappointment as part of human nature.

Joy is delicious perfection. It ignores what's unnecessary. It can take a bad situation and still touch the love that makes it worthwhile. Its test is in your daily distractions. Convenience often accepts an "okay" situation that's far short of your satisfaction. Spiritual accomplishment doesn't mean the sky fills with a thousand rainbows. It means you're always feeling your joy.

Aggressive or laid back, there's something for everyone that gives them joy. It could be your exhilaration riding 80 mph on your motorcycle or enjoying the elegance in a well turned phrase in your favorite poem. And anyone would feel the same joy holding their child's hand. The feeling is the same, but the choice is yours. The details don't matter. Your joy matters. It's important to know it. It's your personality's mastery of love in balance with the world.

Sincerely Yours

Be clear on what you want. Your sincerity helps. Honesty guides you to the truth. Ask yourself what influences you. It's what you were taught and what you learned through experience. It's people's opinions and society's beliefs. You have common sense and your intuition. That's enough to figure things out or totally confuse you.

That's the problem. It's complicated balancing your values and choosing the priority that best fits the moment.

Sincerity means being honest with yourself. It doesn't ask you to be right. It only asks you to *want* to be right. It's your love talking. Even when you aren't right, you can still succeed spiritually. It's an expression of your faith, your trust in love. Being honest with yourself is the only successful policy. If it's emotionally painful, then it means you have a problem. The truth is in your control. You must accept the nature of your situation. Then you can change it to react favorably to your influence.

You can't force change. Consider the martial art, Judo. It controls the force of an opponent's blow by deflecting it away or directing it back on the attacker. It doesn't oppose the force with greater force. It guides the direction of the attack away from its intended purpose and places the opponent in a position to be counter-attacked. You guide the movement. Something pressured against its nature, like a coiled spring, will return to its original shape unless force is continually applied to control it. Force, and its price, shouldn't be necessary if you can guide a change within its nature.

Sincerity is being true to your nature. Your sincerity can identify the changes you need to be happy. There may be an aspect of something that attracts you but overall it isn't good for you, like eating that second piece of cake. It's important to be sincere when you evaluate a benefit if you have to pay too much for it. The important thing is to respect yourself. It can be hard, but if you're sincere you'll find a way. Love is the perfect guide when you're honest.

A sincere soul is a loving soul, but it's tricky when everyone wants something from you. It's normal to be wary of others, even those who love you. You're always responsible to protect yourself. People are so involved in themselves that they often don't consider you till you make it plain to them. That can be uncomfortable. When you're working with superiors it takes tact to respect yourself and respect someone else's authority. You don't want to lose your job. Still, sincerity means honoring your self-respect. You make problems worse when you hide from them, so identify your sincerity and do what you need to have it.

Clarify your clarity.

Life doesn't lend itself to clarity. It lends itself to trends. It doesn't give you much time to consider the details. You barely have time to see the trend. You experience things and form an opinion about them. A good looking person, a nice house, a great car, some celebrity's marriage, who has the most money, a political issue, a disaster, a war, a missing kid, a murder mystery, the local gossip, or some stranger's life on the far side of the world. People's lives are interesting because you share a common experience. That's how you fill the space in your head away from your responsibilities. Your responsibilities are important because they're about your survival. You prioritize them according to your values and balance them with your needs.

Distractions help you feel safe. Entertainment relieves you of your concerns. It helps you focus on inconsequential things because you can't turn yourself off. It could be a hobby, watching TV, gossiping, or any of the distractions current events bring you in the news. Some are harmful, like gambling and taking drugs, but most are okay. It's only a problem if it replaces your responsibility. You balance your responsibilities with your need for relief. Relief supports your soul. Your spiritual welfare isn't just about going to church. It's your comfort anytime you consider your relationship with God.

To counter life's pressures, know what your soul wants. What makes you happy? Get out your pen. Writing things down helps form a picture in your mind to make it easier to qualify. Those qualities are the structure of your happiness. It's not that you don't understand it. It's that you don't give yourself enough time to understand it. Make it a priority. It could be a meditation class or starting a business but take the time to see it. Your soul will show you what you want. All you need is the courage to accept it.

You see yourself in what you can influence. "Influence" because you're assigned your fate. Your world is what you make of it. You don't wave a wand to change things. You negotiate it with God. It doesn't have to be perfect. And it won't cost you more than your sincerity. Whatever you want, you do what it takes to get it. Building anything takes time.

Clarity begins with honesty and your desire to know the truth. It understands how the parts of your life interact. You know how changes create new situations and force you to ask, "Where do I go from here?" You look at everything and question what you need. You want to know everything that affects you. Clarity is the starting point, the "You are here." spot on the map of your life.

Life is simple. You eat. You sleep in a dry place. Relationships are hard. Relationships with family, friends, and colleagues include compromises hidden so deep you usually accept them without even thinking. It's easier. If you want something better, you have to be honest about your relationships. This isn't pointing fingers. This is seeing things as they are. Your sincerity exposes it. It takes courage. It's confrontational even when you don't want it to be. It's emotional and judgmental. That's why you're doing it. You want the truth, not some old habit. Others may not want to change. That's their choice. Clarity is about *you*.

Do you approve?

Respect your responsibilities through an honest appraisal of yourself. You're the only one who can judge what you want. Your dignity expresses in self-approval. Self-approval creates conflicts when it's a matter of fairness. Life's a tug-of-war between self-approval and other people's approval. You want things to be fair without anyone giving up too much.

There's your approval, other people's approval, and the approval you share in agreements. Approval results in permission. It could be accepting a marriage proposal, getting a job, or being approved for a loan. It's not a whim, like what you might think of your neighbor's new car. Approval is an agreement. It's accepting a compromise. You're either born with it or you have to learn how. If you're not sure, ask someone you trust for advice. Advice doesn't replace your approval. It's advice, not an excuse for you to stop thinking. Everyone needs help. You use other people's approval because they may know more than you. It's the mutual respect you need to be a good neighbor. Self-approval is your contribution to a fair bargain.

Approval is part of everything you do. You want to be sure how things work. Approval confirms that you understand it. Approval teaches you safety in an unpredictable world. You constantly ask yourself if you're doing things right, like you were defusing a bomb. It's natural to make judgments, as if you could write better code than God's software. It's your free will. Your judgments are practical but you must appreciate you're a perfect soul with the chance of a lifetime. So approval means you love yourself too.

Self-approval matures. You grow into it. You learn to trust yourself. Whatever advice you get, you're the judge of its value. Self-approval begins with an honest appraisal of yourself. You accept your limits but you also accept you're perfectly able to create your future. Self-approval encourages you because it trusts your sincerity. You don't fear your disappointments. You attempt everything that's reasonable, enjoy your successes, and learn from your mistakes. Every negotiation you face tests your self-approval.

What's your plan?

Planning means thinking. From your dreams and desires it questions your choices. It organizes your thoughts so you can see the whole picture. Your plan makes notes, keeps files, gathers information, and talks to itself. Planning reveals the structure of how to meet your goals. It's rigid in some places and flexible in others. It lets you change it as it develops. Its purpose is your happiness so it continually asks you what you want.

Your desires are revealed in your questions. They expose your foremost priorities. When you envision what you want, your questions focus on it. Your evaluations continue and you question the answers. This process of questions, answers, and more questions is continual. Everything about you advances through your questions. Your questions are your search for universal understanding from your own point of view. You question yourself expecting answers, so answer your questions.

12

Planning organizes your thoughts. It makes change a process. You invest yourself in it. It makes your goals real. It's your questions, actions, and accomplishments, then it starts again with what you've achieved. It identifies your strengths and determines what you need to build up your weaknesses. As your plan develops, it's important to discard the irresponsibility of distractions. If it's worthwhile, keep it. You just don't want to fill your mental garage with useless thoughts.

Your plan should be on paper, a computer file, or something physical that you trust will survive. It frees your mind to consider the possibilities. Don't keep it all in your head where you can forget something. A written plan records it for reference. You're busy. A formal plan makes the pieces easier to chew. You can pay attention to part of it and not worry about the rest. A good plan guides you through the changing relationships. It connects the parts. Anything can be important. It's the old proverb that all your support depends on the weakest link in the chain. Many great fishing trips have been prematurely ended by someone forgetting to put the drain plug in and sinking the boat at the dock.

Your plan can have legal responsibilities. In contracts the wording is crucial. That's why there's redundancy. It's meant to avoid all doubt to its meaning by covering every interpretation. No matter how reasonable you think you are, you have to respect the permanence in a contract. Look at those long-winded statements that come with your software. Click "I Agree." and you're in a contract protected by law. It binds the parties to their agreed responsibilities. You can't change it without a new agreement. When anything has the hint of a legal responsibility, ask an attorney about it. Your plan should always include professional advice to be sure you understand everyone's responsibilities. Don't assume logic will protect you.

Your plan can be complicated when it touches someone else. They have their own interests. Alone, you decide what you do. You can change your plan whenever you like. No one's approval is needed. When you add someone, everything changes. With responsibilities to a child, you have to consider that child's welfare and everything it means. Where a spouse or partner is involved, their interests matter too. You have to satisfy society's plans in zoning, taxes, and traffic laws to name a few. Social rules must be respected if you plan on having friends. It all affects you. It places limits on your plan that you must accommodate to fit in.

Giving & Receiving

Giving and receiving define you. Giving is easy because you control it. You want someone to have something so you give it to them. You want something for yourself so you give it to yourself. It's as simple as that. Within limits, you control your time, money, and sympathies. Receiving is different. It involves someone else's values. You don't control them. Other people exercise control as a personal choice or as an agent of some business or government. They decide if you'll get what *you* want from *them*. You need their permission. All you can do is create an environment that supports them in giving you what you want in the same way you keep your credit clean to make it easier for the bank manager to give you a loan.

You control what others get from you when you decide what you're willing to give. It could mean buying gas where you give your money for the gas being sold. It's the give and take in commerce, the trade that supports your survival. It could be your commitment to take care of an elderly relative unable to care for themselves. In both cases, the choice to give is yours. Physically and spiritually you always want good value. Life has you constantly confronting the dilemma where you have to evaluate the fairness in what you give for what you need.

Regardless of your need, filling it depends on someone else. So know as much as you can about what's important to whomever you deal with. You want them to get what they want so they'll give you what you want. It's usually money or respect. You need money to pay for other things and respect to honor yourself as a human being. Money is a simple negotiation by reasonable people who understand there are other opportunities on both sides. Respect is more important. You might ignore a business deal if you think you're not respected. Self-respect can be the most important thing in the world. Many people would die for it.

Love creates a successful environment for receiving. You receive in negotiations and in gifts of charity. When you receive with grace you

14

give others an opportunity to share their love. It's mutual respect. Respect considers others in the same way you consider yourself. Everyone has an opinion of what makes life successful for them. Considering others creates an environment of trust. You do things for people you trust. Through trust, defenses come down freeing love to bless everyone.

Does love negotiate? Is it manners or kindness? For you it's just a hamburger but for the clerk it's how they make their living. It's important to you both in different ways. You decide the importance of a transaction. Successful relationships require that you respect the other person if you want something from them. Consideration is manners. It eases the friction between strangers. It doesn't ask you for everything. It's not "a matter of life or death" trust. Every situation only requires that you respect the other person so you can respect yourself in your souls' connection to love.

Tell me.

Communication is important, from ordering a taco just the way you like it to making a good impression at your job interview. It's mutual understanding. It's your ability to express yourself so you're understood. It respects your relationships, promotes your interests, and lays out what you expect from others. It respects others' likes, dislikes, resources, and responsibilities. It respects their freedom. You want to be clear what the other person wants even if it's just what temperature to keep the thermostat. It's about mutual comfort. It can be anyone, any age, and any gender. It's the simplest form of cooperation regardless of if you agree or not. All relationships start with communication.

Communication joins you in a common purpose. Everyone needs help. Communication holds the hope that you'll gain something by relating to others. It's the everyday transfer of ideas that tells you the weather, when you'll see a loved one, and the current state of the social condition. It alerts you to opportunities and warns you of dangers. It's your life experience traded with others to inform everyone. It can have a specific purpose as a request or share a general observation that might help anyone. It could be a philosophic musing on human suffering in the hope you can improve it, or, like a joke or gossip, an easy way to pass the time.

Some people talk endlessly about how everything relates to themselves. Others won't talk until you pry it out of them. Most people fall in-between. Regardless of what you're comfortable with, work to improve your communication skills. It may mean talking more. It may mean listening more. Every situation has a moment-to-moment best way to communicate. Adjust your conversation for mutual comfort. Like a jury deliberation, everyone should have their say without having to defend themselves. The best environment for communication will always be a safe place to express your thoughts.

You want to change your life so you talk about it. But the feedback may be negative. That's alright. Every opinion helps clarify the picture. What you hear may not even be about the issue. It could be someone's frightened judgment about life and not have anything to do with you. It could be jealousy from someone's inability to change their own life. People often voice opinions you don't need. Keep those people at a distance where they can't create doubt in your ability. Treat others' fears like a favorite rose bush that needs pruning now and then. Love them, but don't let them block your path.

People are often confronted by a lack of support in their lives. It's part of the social wave you create when you push against the status quo. People will dislike you for being different. They attach their security to social norms that your creativity challenges. Communication helps diminish this threat by exposing the fairness in your creativity. Uninformed people imagine the worst. When you share your hopes, people will identify with you. They'll support you, even with your differences. While your soul's adventure may be unique, everyone has the same desire for happiness.

Communication shares ideas. It's as simple as a yes or no or as complex as a college textbook. It's a thousand articles on spirituality or the memoir of a single life. It's TV advertising, political rhetoric, and a Sunday sermon. It's a birthday card or refrigerator magnet. It's a business seminar or a well-worn sticky note. It's a question in class or a question in your prayers to God. It's the poem you write and the poem you read. It's a badge, a blog, and a sign on a bus. It's small talk, counseling, or a friendly phone call. It's endless. You communicate. It connects you to the world. You're included in the sum of its parts. The world will help you change when it knows what you want. Communicate.

Chapter 2

Down the Road

No education, you cry.

Education means having goals and learning how to meet them. Growing up I didn't have any goals. I wish someone had taught me about them. I guess my parents just expected me to know what I wanted. I didn't. Most of all I didn't realize the importance of making money. I never gave it much thought. It showed up when I needed it. I was never "success" driven. I never had career goals so I never applied myself in high school. I did well when I studied and passed when I didn't. I suffered because my brother was my role model and he was "cool" which basically means he was arrogant, a bad excuse for not doing anything. He wasn't very involved in school activities, not that I knew of. He was too "cool" for that. I never realized how important those activities were for preparing me for the future because I wanted to be "cool" too. But he wasn't very bright. And I didn't know any better.

I rejected my image of high school as not being "cool." The kids who had a purpose got involved. I never thought about being a doctor or a lawyer. I never knew what I wanted. My dad loved basketball so I played basketball. I wish someone had given me better advice. There's not much money in schoolyard games. When I was thirteen my mom took me for psychological aptitude testing. They said I should be a writer. But I didn't have the foresight to train for it.

19

Throughout high school my grades fell until my senior year when I pretty much stopped going. They let me out with a 65 average and I didn't even go to my graduation. Sorry, mom and dad.

I gradually lost interest in school. There were too many distractions in socializing. My senior year was 1967. I became a hippy and started taking drugs every day. I actually got into college with good SAT's and a National Merit Scholarship. I wound up spending 6 months in the cafeteria and dropped out. I had no ambition and couldn't focus through the drugs. I realized I was aimless and, with the help of my parents, a few years later I went to photography school. It turned into four years of part-time work at the United Nations, a great experience working for Mr. Max Machol, the contract photographer for delegates wanting personal photos of themselves. I didn't do much photography after that. Again, if I applied myself I wouldn't have wasted a good opportunity. I just didn't have the confidence. The drugs were easier. I didn't see my mistake until I was an adult and realized that getting an education would have been much easier than taking drugs. I wasted a lot of time with little to show for it.

Action!

Now you do it. You know what you want. You have the right attitude. You checked it out. You weighed the values. You planned for it. You prepared. You did everything the space program does. There's nothing left to do but act. Three, two, one, ignition, and your rocket is off. You committed. You took the step. You made the call. You go there. You meet them. You buy it. You sell it. You make the change.

If you plan well you'll find your support. Still, there's no guarantee. Sometimes you're forced to act before you're ready. Then you'll probably feel uncomfortable. You may hesitate even when everything brings you to the perfect time for a change. It's not easy. There's drama in everyone's life. Success is still your nature. You're entitled to it. As long as you're breathing, you're in the game. Steady yourself the best you can. You'll find courage in your faith.

It starts with an internal negotiation. You ask yourself questions. You evaluate how you'll replace your past with a new design. Your life is like a jigsaw puzzle. You complete an edge to give you a starting point then you fill in the pieces. It's your point of reference for going forward. Like a jigsaw puzzle, you repeatedly look at the cover to remind you what it looks like. You control the disarray by making it match your vision.

Honest considerations don't guarantee you'll make the right decision. Have alternatives. Every value has a different balance. Be ready to promote your interests. You may want a simple yes or no but often you have to accept something you hadn't considered. A positive attitude should be your second nature. Things move quickly. Give yourself room to change. Resist the pressure to rush. Be flexible without yielding what's important. Once you drive that car off the lot it's yours.

You want the unpredictable to be real and reassuring. You want to know you can handle it. You like watching folks on TV doing fabulous things. You want a good life too. There aren't many TV shows where the actors sit around watching TV. Who would watch that? Reality shows aside, who would watch what you do all day? It's a trick question. The only person watching you all day is you. The responsibility for having the life you want is yours.

Every choice you make seeks the right answer. You comparison shop everything. A salesperson seems like your friend when they're selling you something. Ask yourself if they're doing their job persuading you to buy or are they doing you a service explaining the benefits. Is it true when they say, "This is the last one. I don't know when we'll have more." It's possible to miss out on a benefit but it's better to trust yourself and wait if you aren't sure. It's a rare case when you won't have time to consider the alternatives. There's always a new opportunity around the corner. Resist persuasion, even when you're persuading yourself. Act thoughtfully. And be kind to yourself.

Help is on the way.

You have to do it. You have to decide one way or the other. If it makes you nervous, get help. Everyone gets nervous. No one can guarantee a success. No one knows everything. It's your responsibility. Don't expect someone else to do it. Help means

21

assistance. It doesn't mean relinquishing responsibility. Be extra careful in any situation where someone else makes the decision but you're still responsible.

When you ask for help, be clear. It's your plan. It's your goal. You know what it's worth to you. You control it. Help is important where your resources are lacking. It could be time, money, or expertise. It could be a network of friends or one special skill. What's important is knowing how it helps you...and its limits. You don't want it to be an intrusion. And you don't want it to take over your plan.

Help helps you manage your life. It's the friend who helps you move, the handyman who fixes your sink, and the clerk who helps you find what you need at the grocery store. You have a list of service people to help you with skills you don't have. But when you change your life, you're the service person. So you train yourself. You take classes. You practice. You gain experience. And you need friends who inspire you. Like any group of plumbers, the talk eventually gets around to plumbing. Can you do it? Are you confident enough to meet life's challenges, win some, lose some, and still be happy? Of course you are, because with help you can change.

A Trusting Person

Uncertainty begins every endeavor. There are endless possibilities so try not to burden yourself with images of failure. You have to control your fears when you shake things up. The worst things are obvious. For the unknown, all you can do is "Keep your powder dry." Give yourself time. Have money. Be healthy. Create a stable environment with the fewest distractions. Know your choices. Get help from friends. Have realistic goals. Trust your plan. And hope for the best.

Trust yourself you can do this. What if it takes confidence you think you don't have? As disappointing as that is, you grow into your confidence when you stand up to your inhibitions. You can ask the server to double check the bill in a nice way if you think there's an error, but be firm and fair to yourself if there's any resistance. Practice it, whether it's comfortable or not. Your intention is to support your interests not hurt anyone else. Developing confidence means training your mind to trust itself.

You train your mind in the same way you train your fingers to play the guitar. You observe, study, and practice. You accept your mistakes until your fingers follow your thoughts exactly. You identify your bad habits and replace them with good ones. Choose habits that support the person you want to be. Confident beliefs supported by reality become your nature and you'll respect yourself for being the person you are.

Never use success or failure to qualify you as a person. Confidence is your belief in your desires. Confidence is positive but realistic. Confidence must be honest to be dependable. Bravado may be supportive but it lacks sincerity. When you think a lack of confidence is contributing to your problem, accept that you're in training and work things out the best you can. That's part of confidence too. Believe in your success regardless of the circumstances. Respect your beliefs. That's what you're working on. Trust yourself to know right from wrong, whether it's sticking to it or letting go. Never give up on your happiness. Your confidence knows when you're right.

Like Dale Carnegie said, "Until you feel confident, act confident." Know what's right even when you're uncomfortable with it. It doesn't matter if you stumble through it. Everything takes practice. As you improve, don't let the skill in your "performance" substitute for your belief in yourself. You want your confidence to be part of your nature, not part of an act. Keep testing it. Be respectful and express your feelings reasonably when you know someone won't like it. The beauty is how easily you get comfortable with it. Eventually, your confidence becomes part of your personality. Many of your inhibitions aren't caused by your problems. They're caused by your doubts about yourself. You feel that disability. That's the value in confidence. You gain control of your life by accepting your ability.

Self-confidence is spiritual. It comes from self-love. Love connects everything so your support is everywhere. Then why do you have personality conflicts, health problems, delays, things breaking, competition, and the whole gamut of nature interfering with what you want? Because none of it matters. Joy is your harmony with life wherever it takes you. You may be fragile but you do well here. You do well because God supports you. Your faith trusts love. Hope is your belief that love will get you what you want. Charity believes there's value in love. And loving God is your trust in life.

I made a mistake.

What if you get it wrong? Well, you're going to get a lot of things wrong. The question isn't, "What if you make a mistake?" The question is, "Are you willing to do what's needed to succeed?" That includes making as many mistakes as it takes to show you what doesn't work.

Life isn't about being successful at everything. Success is an attitude, not a result. Sometimes you make plans and they succeed. Other times things fall in your lap. Sometimes you fail because you didn't make a good effort and sometimes your best efforts fail for reasons beyond your control. Still, opportunity favors a positive attitude. So why not believe in your dreams? When there's no good reason not to have something, then you should have it.

You just don't want a mistake to waste your time. The time you spend finding out why something failed can be frustrating. You may learn even your goal was a mistake. You want to be honest but judging yourself as part of your mistake is wrong. In reality, a mistake simply helps you reorient yourself towards your goal. Everything contributing to your achievement matters. A mistake is wasted *unless* you use it. A wrong turn can make you look more closely at your map and perhaps you'll find an easier way to get where you're going.

The trap is when you judge yourself by your actions. It's like trying to open a door when you haven't put the key in far enough. The key and tumblers don't line up so you try different positions and jiggle it till the key finds the right position and the door opens. Aligning the key in the lock is not a judgment about your character. It doesn't matter if it takes repeated tries. It only matters that you enter the room. That goes for everything. Life takes a lot of jiggling.

Don't take things personally. You're never a bad person. You're never unworthy. Trial and error educate you. You can't fail. Life is about engagement, not meaningless successes even when they feel good. Failure means not trying. Failure is uncomfortable, but that discomfort is shortsighted. That's why it's important to look for alternatives. Tomorrow is a fresh opportunity. I've learned important lessons late in life. I learned the pain of resentment is my choice every time I seethe at some mindless driver tailgating me. Fix your mistakes...at least in your opinion of yourself.

You want what works for you. Mistakes don't work. If something doesn't help, it's useless to you no matter how important it is to someone else. For me, it's like a bad review. If you use reviews in your advertising, you can only use good reviews. A bad review has no value. You want others to reinforce a good opinion of what you do. But people have their own values. They may not like what you do. I'm grateful when anyone even takes time to review my work. Criticism isn't about mistakes. It's never a true judgment, no matter how superior it sounds. It's just another opinion.

You make more mistakes when you're stressed. The pressure of fatigue can push you past your limit. It can make you incapable of evaluating things correctly. Then you might gamble hoping things will work out. How many times has that made things worse? How many mistakes were avoidable if you only waited till you felt stronger? Comments you shouldn't have made and risks you can't afford can create problems. "Don't drive when you're tired." everyone says. But it's easy to push it when you want to get home. It's never a mistake to admit you're tired and get the rest that helps you to function better. Stress is the pressure you put on yourself. You might feel something's so important that you won't let it go till you burn out on a goal that keeps changing ahead of you. It takes courage to control yourself when you're not ready. Don't worry about failing. Trust that your intentions respect God's love. Love is never a mistake.

Try forgiveness.

Trying something that doesn't work isn't a mistake. It's part of developing your understanding. Everything you do teaches you something. When you're purposeful, it's impossible to make a mistake. It's easy to judge yourself when something goes wrong. Accepting non-judgmental responsibility is a skill you have to learn.

If you were sure about everything, life's mystery would disappear. You love mysteries. That's why you love questions. You want the satisfaction in finding the answers. You want to own the magic in knowing.

Disappointing results are uncomfortable but now you can make a better decision. You learned something. Just redo it. Like Ginger Rogers and Fred Astaire singing, "Pick yourself up, brush yourself off, and start all over again." life wants your best. Whether it's a bird looking for the right twig to build their nest or rain running down a hillside seeking the path of least resistance, trial and error wants what works. You see a possibility and you try it. That's the advantage in advice. You can use someone else's trial and error and save yourself the trouble. Just test it to be sure it's effective the way you want to use it.

Things didn't work out and now you feel bad. You feel guilty because you're the one responsible. It's disappointing, like leaving too late and getting caught in traffic. Disappointments are emotional. When you're calm, you can react calmly. When you're stressed, you react nervously. If you're disappointed with something as important as changing your life it can be endlessly nerve-wracking. Understand that your emotions are powerful forces that must be addressed positively or they'll come back to bite you. Kind words are remembered as support. Angry words are remembered as threats.

Be ready to forgive yourself. The emotional pressure in disappointment eventually passes. Calm down. Don't make a hurried decision to fix things before you're ready. Get your balance back first. Then get back to it. Whatever the problem is, fix it with a clear mind. Your intention is to do your best. Your best encourages you. Self-punishment to enforce your will over your thoughts limits your ability. Your intention to do the right thing is your rehabilitation.

Forgiving others is complicated. People have their own values. When a family member is late to pick you up, you don't like it but as long as it doesn't create a problem you forgive them. Like water under the bridge, it passes by. You know you can count on them in the future.

But what about when a person you don't know lets you down? That forgiveness isn't so easy. It's likely that person never cared about you.

Forgiveness doesn't mean you like the other person or even trust them. It means you respect them. Not personally. It means you respect them as a human being. You accept their nature. God created everything. When you forgive someone, you're really forgiving God. Someone can't forgive you and say, "It's okay this terrible thing you did to me. I forgive you. Sleep well now." Forgiveness isn't a victim accepting an injury. Forgiveness comes from God. If you're ever responsible for something that needs forgiveness, God is where you'll find redemption. If you're sincere in making amends, apologize in your heart and repair what you can. Someone forgiving you doesn't absolve you of your responsibility. Forgiveness releases your humanity so it can be blessed by God's love.

God Almighty!

Through God you control your life. You might ask, "Doesn't God control everything?" That's true. God connects you to everything through love. Then God lets you choose. In the cooperation of billions of people making choices every day you find your balance. Through love and creativity you cooperate with nature. You have resources. Others have resources. The world moves forward in the cooperation of resources, trade. Some opportunities are distributed evenly. Others aren't. Some people have great physical strength while others have cerebral palsy. Most fit in the mainstream. To your soul, they're all opportunities. You express your free will but live in a compromise with society. Even if you want as little human contact as possible, your survival comes from others.

Love controls your life. When you include love in your plans God becomes your partner. Love is the unity in Creation. When you understand everything works together you can be in harmony with it even when you're alone. It's true, "God is love." When you feel love, you're literally touching God. It could be your delight with a friend's success or your peace communing with nature. You become physically whole through the love in your soul. It's your conscious connection to God. Survival is demanding, so love yourself. Separate yourself from life's tasks and invite your soul to join your thoughts, whether it's in your morning prayers or taking a walk on the beach.

God is your greatest resource. God's awareness can show you an easier way. God understands your delays. There are lessons in every experience but it's easy to be confused by unnecessary concerns. God knows this. So God offers its power to you. Not as a conjurer who demands God's performance but as a partner who honors the support in your relationship. Asking God for what you want is your creative beginning. If you've ever had a problem with it, it's because most people do.

Why does God make you struggle when you're doing your best? Isn't your sincerity enough? God sees it, but God explores Creation through your questions. All day long you ask questions. You look for connections and ways to use them. "Is it good?" "Will it work?" "What else could happen?" Questions. Six billion people asking questions every minute. That must mean something. It explains why you're alive. Your creativity asks questions and uses the answers to ask more questions. Through it you explore the mystery of existence, its possibilities, and purpose beyond God's awareness. God wants to know everything so your problems force you to ask questions. Through love, God supports you in it. Problems stink, but love is greater than any problem. Trust love to support your values. Claim your purpose. Claim your life through your questions.

Whether you connect to God through prayer, meditation, or something else, what's important is how you control it. If you don't believe in God, think of it as access to your higher faculties. Either way, it's your decision to employ parts of yourself you can control. People have intuitions, lucky breaks, and bad luck. If you accept that you're connected to natural forces then you can use them. Believe there's a purpose in unexpected events. Look for the value in everything. Things happen for a reason. Positive or not, every experience teaches you something. The patience you learn making an extra trip to take groceries out of the car can save you the time to pick up what you dropped because the load was too heavy. When you accept God's love created the situation, then your love can create the benefit.

There are different ways to argue God's existence. For me, the proof that God is real is the existence of ethics, the consideration that you should be fair to others. Every culture has standards they aspire to as the right way to balance an individual's self-interest with respect for society, not only in public but in their own consciousness. Ask yourself, "Would you lie if you knew you wouldn't get caught?" Most people wouldn't. It conflicts with their self-respect. Self-respect exists in mutual respect. Without mutual respect there's only selfishness. Ethics are the material expression of your love for others. The caring in love connects you to God. Everyone supports everyone, so everybody wins.

Learning

Experience increases your ability to control the unknown. You educate yourself when you respect that. Learning is an odd thing. Sometimes you can figure things out depending on which detail is most important. Other times you go over the same thing again and again until you finally wise up. Some things your antennae are perfectly attuned to and other things you can't see even when they're right in front of you.

Learning can bring you success at whatever you want. Decide what it is and learn how to do it. It's work but it rewards you with knowledge. Instead of uncertainty, you'll find confidence in your expertise. You can do it with anything. You can be a lawyer at any age because the prerequisite is a system of standards. You study the curriculum, pass the tests, meet the standards, and society rewards you with permission to be a lawyer.

You start with a formal education then experience teaches you what works best in which situation. Be alert. Opportunities are everywhere. Take a class or talk to someone who you know has experience. Pay for professional advice or discuss it with a friend. However you continue your education, you respect learning by pursuing it.

Evaluate what you know. Judge it for accuracy, ability, and cost. Be your own teacher. Know when to ask for advice and when to double-check. You need opinions from people you trust. Good intentions aren't enough. You need reliable facts so you can pick your best option.

Respect your sources. There can be conflicting views on the same thing. Eliminate what doesn't feel right. Contact whomever you believe has the best insight on the subject. Ask yourself why you think they should know. If you don't feel right intruding on them; a modest request can do wonders. An intriguing question may get their attention. If that doesn't work, at least you know you've tried everything.

Learning gives you courage when you don't know the answer because it helps you find the answer. Learning gives you knowledge. Knowledge makes you stronger, faster, and more confident. Learning supports your common sense. Your common sense instantly evaluates everything. It considers your moods and beliefs. Learning and common sense teach you how to compromise your moods without compromising your values. It helps you build supportive relationships. In business, making money is everyone's goal. Learning helps you understand the process so the job gets done right and everyone gets paid.

You don't learn common sense. You're born with it. Your daily habits are easy to trust. Unusual experiences are mysteries with possible pitfalls so it's wise to hold back and first get advice. That's your common sense. Some people are smarter than others. Others have a certain affinity for things. Some have more education or experience. Common sense is the equalizer. It's your God-given logic. It's how you relate positively to things that are new to you. It trusts what you know without needing the details. Common sense is your soul's instinct to survive. It's your drive to succeed in everything you do.

Repeat after me.

Maturity means growth. It's the never-ending exploration of your creative self. Creativity means you can change things. You can rework them or try something new. Sometimes a change is unexpectedly forced on you, like getting fired. Other times you plan on it for years, like your retirement. Being caught off guard can be frightening.

30

Waiting years can be frustrating. Your comfort is your attitude toward change. You have to trust yourself that you can handle whatever comes.

Life's familiar. Still, you expect it to change. Your energy level goes up and down. You eat. You get energy. You work. You get tired. You rest. Your energy returns. Parts of you grow. Parts of you die. All this as you constantly compete in life's grand interaction. Life moves. It explores. It grows. It procreates. It dies. Your creativity reorganizes what nature has started. You graduate school and plan a career. You seek a mate and marry. You go to work and have a life. A storm knocks your house down or a distant uncle leaves you a fortune. Change moves your life along. Once you make a change, you want more changes. You aspire to travel, raise a family, or get a more rewarding job. That's your nature. Your whole life is preparation for your next change.

When you're engaged in something, time disappears. You live in your attention. At that moment, you choose what's important to you. The changes you control you do easily. The changes you negotiate need attention. You need others' support and God's support. Time disappears in negotiations because comparing values is important. God's plan must be considered. Still, your free will gives you choices. Balancing your desires with God's plan is the joy in negotiation. Time can always wait.

Life is a balance of your ambitions, resources, and responsibilities. You're born with the ability to make it whatever you want. All you have to do is shift your attention. Like taking a train to a new destination, you throw the switch that sends your train onto the next track. You control it. Sometimes the whole system has to change, like when you move to a new city. Other times, changing one feature, like a new job, is enough to change everything that grows from it. Growth is more than development. It precedes a new direction.

What will you do today? Will you plug yourself into some old routine or try something new? Routines are useful. You can create something interesting or change it as you go. You decide. Life's not just about solving the problems you run into. It's about creating the problems

31

you want to solve. You choose the repetition of events. You wake up and wash your face each morning. Where that is, who you're with, and how you do it is up to you. You thrive with other opportunistic souls in the same competing cycles. Just think "rush hour." But like everyone else, you get past it and do your best to enjoy the things that make your life interesting.

So Much Pressure

To anyone new, you're an unknown. So people size you up by your appearance. Are you a homeless person or an executive? They'll see who you're with and what you're doing. In introductions, they'll ask about your job, your family, and your interests. They want a feeling for your attitude towards life. What are your values? What can you do? Can you be trusted?

They'll decide if it's worth it to know you better. They'll see something they like, or not, and create a relationship accordingly. From your perspective, you'll decide the relationship you want with them. Maybe you'll find something in common. Other times you'll meet someone so repulsive you can't wait till they leave. You'll find this and everything in-between as the circumstances decide your compromises. This isn't only about new people. It could be a family member or neighbor. As you grow, you can become a new person to someone you already know.

A family member appreciates your growth. They've watched you mature through your ups and downs. But a change can surprise an acquaintance you've only known a short time. They've already adjusted to you a certain way. Now they have to come up with a new standard that respects who you are now. This can happen when you're promoted to a position of authority over someone you previously worked with as an equal. Now, instead of support, you might be seen as a problem.

You learn to accept your disappointments and still love yourself. Relationships are harder. Too many unknowns with other people deciding what's best for themselves. Then the uncontrollable risks can be a strain. "Don't drive in the rain." you plead to a loved one. But everyone has their own values. The pressure comes when you see someone you love whose values are out of balance. There you have the least control. You can give advice but you can't make their decisions for them. So you're always under pressure balancing your responsibilities while you keep an eye on the ones you love.

Good friends will encourage you. They'll help you in ways you didn't expect. But pressure creates instability. Wanting a new balance for yourself may be the opening for your friends to talk about how they admire what you're doing. The opposite is true too. Acquaintances may feel jealous; guilty they haven't found the courage you have. A friend will stand up to the pressure with you. Love stands up to everything. Your real friends will be happy for you whether they understand you or not. "Okay. Great! You've evolved." You chose what you wanted and risked it. Now your future beckons with the thought your new life is possible with everyone you love on board. While the pressure of wanting good opinions is real, your success is in loving yourself.

Chapter 3
You're in Charge

The Aimlessness of Drugs

I was a drug addict from 1966 to 1974. I really didn't stop taking drugs until around 1980. There were odd jobs but I basically spent my time looking for drugs and getting high. I lived with my parents half the time and bounced around New York City where I had decent luck finding cheap apartments. My life changed in 1974 when I was able to hold a steady job driving a taxi. It was a catch-all job for people like me who liked their independence. That was the start of me getting off drugs. When I showed my father I could keep a steady job he let me work in his printing company and I finally joined society. I did less and less drugs because I needed them less. Taking drugs was a crutch. It was easier than facing my insecurities when I was straight.

I lived in a quintessential New York studio apartment, fifth floor walk-up, tub in kitchen, with a huge skylight on west 29th Street between Fifth and Broadway, no A/C, just a big fan I kept on the floor. I paid $165 a month including electric. It was an industrial area, barely anyone lived there. It was also safe because no one lived there. It wasn't close to anything so it was also very lonely. It was desolate at night and on the weekends. But it was just a ten minute walk to work. I lived there four years and it changed my consciousness. I spent my time rebuilding my life. I saved my money. I healed my thoughts. In the middle of the busiest city in America I removed myself from civilization. And I got better.

It was my cocoon and my catharsis. I had created my own half-way house. I gradually stopped taking drugs and entered the real world. The funny thing about healing from drugs is once you don't need them your enthusiasm returns. I had suffered a mental injury for 16 years and now I was on the mend. I spent my time reading self-help books and getting to know myself. I learned about negative thinking. By then my whole thought process was negative thinking. I learned to identify my negative thoughts and set about removing them from my consciousness, the most liberating thing I've ever done. It took me two years of constant effort, literally every waking moment through repetition changing my negative thoughts into positive ones. It was stressful but I did it. It's a miracle how negative thoughts diminish until they finally disappear. Thank you, God.

Fear is a friendly warning.

Fear comes from a belief that you're *helpless*. It's a lack of trust in your ability to protect yourself. It's your belief that there's nothing you can do and you'll be lost, empty, and alone. Then missing your flight isn't just inconvenient. Fear makes you think you'll lose everything. Fearlessness isn't in your will. It's in your faith. While your will motivates you to overcome obstacles, faith leads you to succeed any way you can. Faith attracts God's attention. With faith, you don't need defenses. If faith is trust in love and God is love and there's nothing greater than God, then there's nothing to ever worry about.

You're it!

Accept your leadership role. When you see yourself as the person responsible for your life, you empower yourself. Your power always comes from you regardless of your place in life's hierarchies. You're the commander of who you are. You decide what you do with your life. You can compromise when it's in your best interests or look for a better deal somewhere else. Encourage yourself. Born leaders are rare but you have the inclination. Nurture it. Make it part of your character. Become a dependable steward of your life. Leadership is your freedom and you'll never be comfortable without it.

When you ignore your responsibilities you're at a disadvantage. It's frightening to be unsure of yourself. But when you defer, others will direct you to serve *their* interests. You're always responsible for your life. Others can only give the appearance of directing you. It's your choice to follow. Responsibility is a fascinating ride because the results always come back to you.

You become a better leader through experience. You don't have to know all the answers. You should always seek advice. Sometimes whatever you choose will have a downside. That's the difficulty in being a leader. You're responsible for the result. Leadership is more than enjoying the respect of those around you. It's giving the respect that requires you to step up and make difficult decisions that affect others. Leadership means controlling your urge to retreat, keeping a positive attitude, and making a decision. Then you move on. Like pedaling a bicycle, forward or backward, the cycle of the chain never ends. It's just a matter of changing gears.

You really don't have a choice. You're always responsible for yourself. If you're confused, don't worry. Leadership is a prized trait. It's important to having a successful life. That means there's guidance everywhere. You'll find everyone has a story about how they made a difficult decision and what they learned. You're responsible for your leadership skills so take the wheel. If you're concerned you might make a mistake, then you're on the right track. From the airline pilot to the gardener, everyone makes mistakes. "I'll never do that again." you say. And, hopefully, you won't. The worst mistake is to ignore the lessons in your mistakes. Respect your errors for their benefits. You can't control how the Universe reacts. You can only control how you react.

More Training

Decide that you want leadership skills as part of your character. Watch others. How do they accept responsibility? How do they deal with conflicts? How do they talk to their superiors and subordinates? When do they delegate? When do they jump in? When do they ask for help? How do they create cooperation? How do they deal with opportunities? Where do they find alternatives? What are their values? Are they honest? How do they balance their decisions with respect to what they want, what it costs, and the others involved? How successful are they? Why?

You won't run out of chances. You're always deciding something. Ask yourself, "Why are they doing that? Is it being responsible? If they didn't accept responsibility what would happen?" Insightful questions reveal the true values. "Are they asking about others or preoccupied with themselves? How important are their concerns? Are their values sensible under the circumstances?" Then relate it to yourself. Make your judgments. Develop your own sense of responsibility.

Apply your values. When you hear people arguing, you know when they're being sensible or fighting over nothing. Compare it to an attitude you believe accepts responsibility. Be generous. You never know all the facts. See how others act when you understand their options. The treat is when you see someone accept responsibility, decide they can respect themselves, and be fair too. That's control. That's what you want for yourself.

You come face to face with responsibility when someone has authority to make decisions that affect you, like the government or an employer. You may feel they deserve a say for the sake of keeping order or they don't know anything and it's a wonder how they got to where they are. You learn responsibility by watching others. From the safety of your thoughts you can judge why someone agrees to what they're doing. You have an opinion of what responsible decision-making is and you can watch the process play out to see if it matches your opinion. It's a cheap education that you don't have to pay for yourself.

You teach yourself leadership. You know people say, "There's no such thing as a dumb question." Well, they're wrong. There are dumb questions. Any question you first haven't considered yourself is a dumb question. You're not dumb so don't take the easy way out. Don't avoid thinking. You know what you want more than anyone else. Before you have someone answer a question for you, think about it in relation to your values. Then refine your question into an answer that serves you.

Learn the ins and outs of leadership. Business and the military demand these skills. If you don't have them, those are great places to learn. Take classes. Surf the net. There are more opportunities than you need. Get experience. Volunteering is a great way to develop leadership skills. See what attitudes others use successfully. Learn to work with a team to achieve your goals. Being a leader doesn't mean you're perfect. It means you accept responsibility and you're willing to grow into it.

No More Excuses

You know what you want. At least you should want to know. You know what you like, what you don't like, and if you have it or not. You know your situation if you're honest with yourself. You have many purposes, just like a big city with its constantly changing issues and infinite details. You decide what you like. It isn't important why it matters to you. It's only important that you have it. It solves old problems and creates a satisfying new reality.

You have an idea of the changes you need to make it happen. You build a base from your decisions. You gain a sense of yourself, your dignity. You have values. You have the self-respect that demands your values be respected. Encourage your ideals. Defend them. Like a rock band, success is a competition of harmonies yielding to a common call. Six billion souls have the same thoughts you have. Respect your dreams. Fairness frees society to benefit everyone...including you.

Be clear about your purpose. Appreciate it needs attention. It's not a fixed entity. It moves with nature's gyrations, society's whims, and your own human hungers. Keep your happiness on track. Whatever happens, make the best of it. Your goals change as you learn life's limits. Your maturity brings you new opportunities. Sometimes it's a chance to experiment. Other times it's a chance to eliminate something holding you back. Whether or not you have it, your happiness will guide you to it.

When things don't work, try to think clearly. Confusion and disappointment are intimidating barriers. They make you feel weak. That's when you have to work harder or let go. Your support is your ability to think positively. The same kindness you give to a stranger you should give to yourself. That includes the time to rest and refocus. Coming to terms with failure is exhausting. Your goals are still the same. The same exuberance you started with is still there, but it may need rekindling. Accept life's timing. Bless your soul with good character and a positive attitude. Your physical situation has little to do with your soul's success. Love and sincerity define you.

A free society offers you many paths; ways to support yourself and find love and contentment. Love is your motivation. Some societies prize self-reliance. Others extol commitment to an ideal. The attitude that supports the solitary rancher is different from the constant interaction between strangers in a big city. Personal responsibility is its core. You agree with the social contract, change it, or live somewhere else. You're always an individual in whatever society you choose. You have responsibilities to yourself and to your neighbors. Your soul balances on love. That's the only place you'll ever find peace.

You decide.

Where are you going for lunch? Who will you marry? What will you do for the rest of your life? Most choices are insignificant. Others change everything. Some are free. Others cost you all you have. Decisions matter. It's unusual for a choice to change everything without a chance to change it back. God's blessing is that life *usually* gives you time to change your mind. Even though you want it now, life doesn't rub a lamp and a Genie pops out granting you your wish. No one wants problems but, like it or not, problems build your character. They prove love's power. Love's the most valuable thing you have. Creativity expresses love in so many ways so you'll find ones you like.

Decisions are important. If you feel uncomfortable making them, learn how. Everyone's making hard decisions. Consider the result. Your decision creates something new. You want it to be a benefit.

Your decisions affect others. When you change your place in line, everyone has to move to make room for you. That change can be important to someone who doesn't have any interest in changing. Be considerate. Everyone's bouncing around even if you don't see it. Everyone's resources are different. Disrupting someone's stability can be testing. Be respectful. Be clear so others can adjust to you without having a major problem.

That's not always possible. You have a responsibility to yourself first. Everyone has their own values. Honor your self-respect but accept that not everyone shares your values. Everyone reacts differently. You won't be happy with all your choices either. Leadership is personal. You're looking for the best choice, not a perfect one. Mitigate the unfairness as best you can, but decide. When you respect everyone, hopefully they'll respect you back.

Trust you'll make the right decision. What's right is always a balance of cost and consequence. The key is how well you work under pressure. Will your evaluations be rushed or can you patiently weigh the values and make the right decision. Time helps but life isn't always accommodating. You don't want to miss the train. The world may run 24/7 but you go by workdays, weekends, and delays. You have others to consider too. You have to respect the social clock. You have appointments and schedules to meet. Part of every decision is to ask yourself, "Do you have time to question your decision and still meet your responsibilities?"

Focus your attention and you'll do a good job. Assign priorities. Develop a process. Things take their own time. You may be pressured by others' insistences. Demands are distracting. They split your attention between what you want and protecting yourself from a conflicting agenda. It's how you share your time. Maybe someone won't give you time. They want what they want and don't care about you. You don't have to win every argument. You have to stand your ground when it matters, keep your faith, and let the chips fall where they may.

Turn off the static. Only listen to those you trust. Take your time. You may need a minute or a month. Think things through. Even those who love you can only judge you from their point of view. Those close to you may know you, but not everything. Confirm your beliefs. Keep a healthy skepticism. No one's right all the time. Make the advice convince you. Accept responsibility. Any choice you make sensibly has the best chance to succeed.

Examine your options. "Is everything where you want it to be? Can it be improved? Is everyone doing what you want them to do? Do you feel you have control? Is the current flow favorable or is something more needed? Have you looked at everything? Do you need help?" And that's not even the details.

While your situation may seem stable, your options keep changing. Conditions change. People change. Your desires change. Each of them affects you differently. Still, the basic question remains, "How can you make things better?" Then, "What else can you do?" It's not important to have an immediate answer. You want a practical answer. Like shopping for a new car; you pick the model and price, then you negotiate the financing and extras. You compromise because you have priorities. Every feature may not be available. You may find it cheaper at another dealer. You double check, then you say "Yes!", sign the papers, and drive away in your new car. This process applies to every part of your life and it always starts with what you want.

Let's cooperate.

You rarely make a decision that affects only you. It's not like you're lost alone in the woods in a foreign country. If you don't show up, someone's going to look for you. People know you; friends, family, acquaintances, even strangers. You affect people. They affect you. It means cooperating. People cooperate when they see working with others helps them. They might see it as helping you because they love you or they like you because you share a common interest, like coming from the same hometown. They may just want to do business with you. It's all fine. In cooperation, it's still up to you to be the visionary, coordinator, salesperson, and cheerleader. At the same time, maintain your oversight to be sure everything goes as planned.

The key is communication. You have to let people know what you want from them. You have to relate a fair expectation of what it's going to cost them, how long it'll take, and what they'll get in return. There's always an exchange of time, money, effort, and opportunity even when your payment is the love you share in friendship. People will decide if cooperating with you is worth it. Most people are generous. They just want to be treated fairly.

People will cooperate as long as they believe they matter to you. Your consideration is returned with the cooperation you need. Cooperation means someone helps you when you need them and you help them when they need you. There can be a conflict when expectations differ. It's important to be clear as soon as something changes. Circumstances naturally evolve. They improve, deteriorate, or become a new plan. Honesty creates trust. You respect the trust in cooperation by creating respectful agreements.

People cooperate because it's in their best interests. Teammates on sports teams, performers in the theater, or people in any profession may hate each other, but their self-interest finds cooperation is the way they'll succeed. Conflicting views can both be right. Personal priorities change the values. Sometimes one view is right. Another time the other view is better. As long as you can see the situation from the other person's point of view you can make sure everyone's interests are respected. You respect yourself when you appreciate there are times you should cooperate. Cooperation is a negotiation where everyone works together to achieve their own goals.

Yea! Team

Everyone will look to you for guidance. You started this. You know your goal. You have an idea of what you need and what it'll cost. You see the big picture. At least, you see the immediate picture. Often the people helping you will have more expertise than you. They can show you the pitfalls in your plan. It's your job to explain how their knowledge helps you. It's up to you to assign responsibilities according to who's the most capable. Give them an appreciation of what you need so they can weigh the values from your point of view.

Don't think you have to micromanage everything. It's up to you to find people who can solve problems without you looking over their shoulder. It's important that they know you trust them so they'll trust themselves. Communicate your goals and what you expect. Let them know your priorities and how their contribution helps you. When you're presented with options; confirm what's needed, prioritize your needs, then do what's needed.

Anyone who does work for you, you want them to do well. They're on your team. When a problem comes up, you want them to work with you to find ways to solve it. Encourage them to do their best. You want the most experienced to do their best and the least experienced to do the best they can. Respect everyone according to their ability. Treat everyone fairly. Everyone needs help. When people trust that you care, they'll be reliable and you'll reap the benefit.

Lead the team. Clarify the situation. Find out what's missing. Respond sensibly. Show confidence. Demonstrate your ability. Your attitude is contagious. Project a positive outlook. You don't need all the answers. Understand the problem and deal with it step-by-step. Communicate what you're doing, why you're doing it, and what you expect from them. You want everyone to take advantage of working as a team.

Your team includes the butcher, the baker, the candlestick maker, (and now maybe your internet provider.) They may not know it. It's your job to tell them. Identify your team. Work relationships, social commitments, your contacts with strangers, professional relationships, merchants, and the government are all your orchestra. You're the conductor. Understand the psychology of personal dignity, personal purpose, and how cooperation is essential to managing your team. You are the team. The team must be respected along with its individuals. Everyone expects it. Though you give excellent directions, like a chorus line, they synchronize themselves. When they trust you, depend on them. When they doubt you, you're alone.

Trust creates the synergy in cooperation. Two people can lift a weight one person could never lift by themselves. A team relies on everyone contributing to the goal. There's always self-interest in a common purpose. Regardless of the personalities, there's a thread of trust that rises to serve that purpose. The point of teamwork is you don't have to do everything yourself. Your team looks out for your interests even when you're not there. They just want respect. They want to be certain whoever you delegate your authority to also has their interests in mind. Your trust in their ability shows your respect. If you don't feel it, you might as well find someone else. People know when you don't trust them. And that's enough for them not to trust you.

Some people excel at certain tasks. Your job is to encourage everyone to do their best, consider how it benefits the team, and work through the problems without blaming anyone. The team supports everyone. It's conscious of everyone's contribution and supports its weaknesses. Everyone should be conscious of how your team's integrity is supported by the welfare of each member. That's your job, to keep them healthy, happy, and moving forward towards your goal. With purpose and confidence, people are wonderful working together. They'll do well as long as you lead them. Everyone you meet is a potential teammate in one way or another.

Show me what you got.

People matter. Time matters. Money matters. You need them all. One creates the others. Your time, love, and money are your power. They exist in nature, which you can't control, so you have to work with nature. When you respect the natural rhythms of events, from the changing seasons to your own breath (Think how distracting a tight pair of pants can be.), nature will give you room to build your life with the resources you have.

Take inventory. Count your relationships, skills, talents, interests, education, finances, possessions, opportunities, health, and spirituality. You'll need them all. Know what's lacking. You don't need a plan for every detail. There's always the unexpected. Some things won't be available. Others will fortuitously pop out of nowhere. Be keen to your surroundings. Know how you'll support yourself in every situation.

Examine your situation. What does your plan need to succeed? How will you track it? Will you keep it all in your head working through old situations as you plan new ones? That can be overwhelming. You don't want to miss anything. Writing things down is enough to bring order and *relief* to your mind. It can be a detailed progression or a jumbled scribble just to spark your thinking. List the details. Prioritize them. Keep thinking about everything. Specify what connects each detail. Assign tasks. Like the CEO of a big corporation, your responsibility is tracking the plan and making sure everyone's on board. So you constantly need information. You need advice on everything. Don't make your plan a secret but be discrete and protect it. Trusting people is a challenge because everyone has their own agenda.

Your main asset is you. Little should happen without your oversight. Others may help, but they can only give what they *think* you want. Their best intentions have limits. It's their creativity. Their ideas may not fit your plan. Be an active leader. You'll need a clear mind so avoid unnecessary burdens. The commotion of an evolving plan needs good guidance. You know when you're feeling good or not. Be patient enough to respect your well-being if you care about your future.

Every business advertises how important their employees are to giving you good service. From the parking lot attendant to the bank loan officer, positive relationships make life easier. People matter. Respecting others in the same way you respect yourself is the golden rule of fairness. People respect and protect themselves. When you show you respect them too, they'll trust you. They'll accept you as a partner and do what they can to help you as long as they believe they're being treated fairly.

Money affects everything. When you need something, you buy it. You survive by trading the value you produce for the value someone else produces. Money is the common denominator. Anything you want can be described by the money it costs. That's a $20,000 car or it's a million dollar house. Living is continual so your need to pay for it is continual too. Like a forest squirrel, you need to eat every day. Value is determined by need. Price is determined by availability. Side issues can affect the price like when you need something right away or you want to give a good deal to a friend. A real sense of value comes from experience. If you need to know what time it is, a good watch works just as well as a pricey one.

Time is odd because it's both endless and limited. It's endless because it's infinite. It's limited because you organize your life according to the schedules you create. Eternity has no measurement. You manage it through "time." "It's a week's work." Or, "It's almost Spring." It's natural. You identify nature's cycles and human schedules by the time they take. It could be a thirty second stop light or the two hundred year lifespan of a tortoise. When the energy changes, things take on a new character whether it's time to step on the gas or the death of the tortoise. It could be the summer vacation you look forward to or the admonition to work hard in the saying, "The early bird catches the worm." Time is a process. You control it like a river. You build the dams, canals, and every other structure that keeps it taking you where you want to be.

There's no situation beyond your understanding. Things make sense even when you don't like them. Your options may be limited but you know where you are and what you want. Your emotions guide you to what you think is good for you. Your thoughts identify the facts, assign values, and prioritize them. Your imagination connects your thoughts to create opportunities. Everything you do begins with a thought so be honest with yourself. Your thoughts are your interpretation of life. Your spirit supports your thoughts as it questions its purpose. The creative process means, like an artist, you can change things.

God is your bounty. Put aside religion. If you don't believe in God I think you're looking unrealistically at love. If you expect the world to have your values, it's your personal belief in what you think life should be not what it is. When you see life for what it is, you'll see every challenge has a set of questions and answers that make sense. They're insights into your soul, its achievements and miseries. Eventually you die and your problems disappear. Eternally, "Every cloud has a silver lining." Certain things you can only learn through pain. Nobody likes it. At least, learn what it means for you. If you ask, God will show you how. Sympathy and compassion serve love too.

Is it worth it?

No one knows what you want better than you. You decide what has value to you. Your priorities support whatever serves that purpose.

You know what you want but you can't be sure what will happen. Life's a road you've never driven on with turns you can't foresee. You prepare the best you can. You have to believe whatever happens you'll deal with it...even if it's cleaning up a mess. Your comfort is your confidence and perseverance. If you ever find your goal lacking, change it. You're never bound by anything other than your happiness. No matter what you consider, its test is how it serves you.

You're not alone. What you value is valued by others. They're your competition. You can draw a circle around your friends and family, the people you care about. Their welfare is important to you even when they have little say in your choices. You're generous with them. You can deal with strangers the same way. Find out what they want and what you can do for them. You can respect and love them, be fair, and still negotiate in your best interests. It's finding the point of value where all parties see a benefit and agree to trade. Between love and survival there's always room to bargain.

There are things beyond the price that make a deal attractive. A deal starts with trust. When you're fair and honest, your chances improve that you'll get what you want. You create value by finding alternatives, knowing when adding something presents a better deal. What would help the other trader and not cost you too much? What would you get in return? All values fall into simple categories: price, convenience, service, features, quality, selection, delivery, and intangibles like throwing in tickets to a ball game. Leave the core negotiation alone. Nibble on the benefits at the edges. Where a service includes products and labor, the labor is a fixed cost to the merchant. The merchant has those costs whether you buy from them or not. That can be adjusted. Your car mechanic may throw in a free tire rotation to sweeten the deal. They make money on the tires they sell you and they want you coming back. Bargaining creatively means creating a new balance of values. That's why it's called an art.

It's natural to give your opinion. Whether it's your experience at a new restaurant or advice on getting a job, it's normal to support others with what you know. Typically, advice is caring. But it can be self-serving as you might find in a business deal where negotiations include the formality of friendship but the focus is really on making money. Examine suggestions carefully. Some people are just impressed with their opinion of themselves. Others have valuable advice even when they charge for it. Paying attention is the cheapest advice of all. It answers the same question you've asked since you were born, "How do you do that?" Everyone contributes a unique point of view. Advice only asks that you use your common sense. Getting good value goes with every goal. In the end, you sell yourself on what's best for you. You compare endless opinions to the point of saying yes or no, then the future will show you how well you did.

Who could do better?

There's too much to do by yourself, too many specialized tasks. You need help. You need people you trust to do things for you. There's always an element of uncertainty, especially when you use young people with limited experience. Young people will usually do the job cheaper because they're competing with experienced workers. That's the trade-off. You have to pay closer attention. You don't want to be involved in every decision. You do want to be confident the job gets done right. The balance between cost and confidence is unpredictable. As mundane as it seems, dealing with everyday uncertainties is the core of the mystery that builds trust in your faith.

Choosing the right person includes their education, experience, skills, talents, temperament, time, cost, and if they have the tools you need. You want the best one for the job. Love connects you even in a business relationship. If not, everyone would be a hermit. Make the job easier. Be ready to add resources and ideas. You want everything done right. After all, it's for you.

Comparing competing ads in the phone book feels like walking through a minefield. You're never quite sure where to step. You review the ad, weigh the costs, throw the dice, and employ someone you don't know who you think could help you. Just be ready to take over. Get involved when you see you're needed. Don't over-manage experienced people but even the best tradesperson can have a bad day. Let them do their job before you go looking for problems. Still, be sure your doubts are resolved. Regardless of the cost, you can always find someone else. Be open-minded and, hopefully, you'll be happily surprised. Even more, you'll know better next time.

Getting help gives you time to lead. You can use an accountant instead of beating your brains out over your taxes. The task doesn't matter. In sports, every season starts with everyone eyeing the championship. Hopeful rookies join seasoned veterans. You're the manager. You want everyone to do well. You know the meaning of winning. You know what's needed. You encourage your rookies while you trust your veterans have another good year in them. The formula changes as you deal with injuries and practice pays off on the field. Your job is to keep the team's creativity focused on *your* goal. People think of themselves constantly. Combining your players' values is the skill. Like making a clay bowl, you add a little here, take away a little there. Don't call every play. Just be ready when you have to.

Don't give up. Change things.

Success can take longer than you think. Your plan may fail. New problems come up. Your road swerves into unknown territory. Trust your commitment. Whether it's perseverance or faith, you need a kernel of commitment to support you when things get tough. It's fun to ride your enthusiasm when things go well but social conflicts, a lack of resources, natural events, and even fate can create obstacles. It's not your fault. It's your responsibility. You're doing that now. By reading this book you're encouraging yourself to succeed.

Decide, whatever happens, you'll go forward. Review your goals. Should any be eliminated? Your plan isn't your purpose. Your happiness is your purpose. Looking back, you can see what wasn't important. Your courage may be admirable but a battle isn't always your best choice. Getting help, taking time, or admitting something isn't working doesn't mean you're not committed. The pace of your progress isn't spiritually important. Your humanity may be frustrated but your soul shrugs it off and holds to its purpose with superhuman strength. You may be suffering, but life questions your soul. The sooner you learn what it wants, the happier you'll be.

Whether it's your best friend or the pizza delivery person, people see your attitude as your opinion of them. Be conscious of the signals you send in your voice and body language. Like the saying goes, "You catch more flies with honey than with vinegar." Instill others with trust in your support. A self-centered attitude offers, at best, the shadow of cooperation, not the spirit. Explanations are less convincing than your enthusiasm. It could be your positive outlook or your willingness to return a favor. You motivate others through your feelings. If you ever send the wrong message, fix it as soon as you can. Your supporters will accept the adjustment and respect your judgment.

Show you're committed. Let your disappointments pass. Have positive ideas. Act confidently. Don't identify with the obstacles. Release your resentments and rationalizations. Remember the tribulations in your victories but don't lean on them. Know when to move on. Unless you find problem-solving fun, like some video gamer, commit your energy to winning everything.

Endless, Endless, Endless...Possibilities

You're creative but you have limits. Within those limits you choose a direction. You set goals, create relationships, and assign values. But decision-making is more than choosing from what you know. You can create things that never existed before. Your knowledge expands nature's limits. Limits come from distrusting your imagination. Creativity is your ability to make limitless combinations from existing ideas. Every time you learn something, your inventory of possibilities should be re-examined. "If only..." is a working reality. Like the art student contemplating the old master, your creativity renews itself from what you learn.

You control your creativity by asking questions. When a mechanic sees a machine not working, they look for anything out of place, any unusual sound or smell. They look for anything that might be the cause. Your creativity begins your questions with what you know and

51

respects there are things you don't know. Like the mechanic, you can tighten a screw or replace a worn part to bring it back into alignment. But your creativity lets you look at something doing well and ask yourself, "How can you make it do better?" Then the mechanic in you becomes an inventor. If there's a way to improve it, you'll find out how.

Be a scientist. It's not as strange as it sounds. Science measures how things react under different conditions. You use science by finding the consistencies in nature, the limits you can rely on. It doesn't mean you're good at math or chemistry. It means you examine things to see how they function. You want to know what to expect and how to control it, including people. You size them up. You measure their reactions. You do it all the time. Like when you hire a plumber. Did they bring the right tools with them? Or, do they mumble discontentedly when they learn you live in a five floor walk-up?

Be an artist. Art is your imagination. If you don't feel anything special about painting and music, question it. Art teaches you to use your imagination to question your environment. As an artist your imagination is your tool. It's not about paints and sounds. It's about ideas. It's exploring new possibilities. Art reveals your soul to your mind. Your job is to respond. Mix and match, poke and pull, change things to find ways that touch your soul. Maybe you weren't born with artistic talent. You can still share an artist's attitude to create. Art connects your soul to your imagination. In the process, you become God's partner.

You can think of yourself as a loving soul, a work of art, or a scientific equation. Whichever you choose, you improve yourself through your questions. Your creativity takes every point of view to find new opportunities. Keep asking yourself, "If I do this, what happens?" "If that happens, what happens next?"

You're really all of them; scientist, artist, and priest. Those are your job titles for asking questions. It's God's purpose so it's your purpose. God uses your questions to understand itself. No other creature has the free will to do this. Some animals appear to be creative but it's really a natural talent they use to survive. You use your creativity to survive. Human beings lived in caves until they realized they could build a shelter closer to the river. Your questions reflect God's nature. Through nature, God creates opportunities for your questions. There's the argument that apes have 98% the same DNA as human beings so human beings are simply evolved apes. Does that mean if you write a hundred songs an ape can write ninety-eight? Of course not. It's obvious there's more to it than your DNA. You're different in your being. You have the free will to choose. Like dieting, you don't have to accept your body's hungers. You ask questions and create new things. God loves new things. You do too, even if it's just a new set of tires.

You have more control when you're creative than when you wait to react to an unknown situation. In the creative process you can always find a new idea. It's your choice to use your creativity. The world is your adviser so look for the spark of usefulness in everything.

Chapter 4
The Next Hill

Mental Illness

I started seeing psychologists when I was fourteen years old. I was rebelling against my immaturity and my parents didn't know what to do. By the time I was twenty I was in a mental hospital. The conflict between my intelligence, my inability to effect anything positive in my life, my negative emotions, and taking drugs put me in a self-destructive tailspin that resulted in my mental illness. Through the grace of God and my parents I survived. They couldn't show me how to live but they stood by me through the bad times. I wound up in South Oaks Hospital on Long Island for two months in the summer of 1970.

I was constantly afraid. It got to the point I was having auditory hallucinations. It was my negative thoughts talking to me. I did a full series of insulin and electric shock treatments. Then the symptoms of Hepatitis C showed up and they rushed me to a general hospital. I contracted it three months earlier and the disease takes 90 days to incubate. I was in isolation for two weeks and I almost died. Another two weeks and I was free but I still can't give blood today. I'm grateful to my parents. I think the shock therapy helped and my time at South Oaks broke me of some dangerous habits.

I improved. The worst confusion of my mental illness was over but it was a long way back. The war in Vietnam was raging and I wasn't in school, prime draft material. In 1968 I was classified 4F, not fit for military service. My psychological problems had kept me out. It was a good thing. I don't think I would've lasted a day.

Moving Past The Past

You're not always going to be right. You might choose the wrong thing for the wrong reason. Or, you'll do everything right and it doesn't work out. All you can do is increase your chance of success. You can't guarantee it. You hope the machines you depend on work, which they don't always do, or the people you work with perform as you expect. What you think is fair and reasonable might be rejected. Your greatest ally may not be available. You might be in a bad mood and make a wild decision or get caught in a stupid mistake, like falling asleep and missing your plane. Anything can happen. Train yourself to be comfortable with unpredictable anxieties. It's part of life's landscape. Stability is a good friend but fickle when billions of people are competing with nature.

Move past your disappointments as painlessly as possible. The intimacy of a failure is tough to wrestle with but try not to beat yourself up. A problem is real. It has to be fixed. Your plan didn't work so learn from it. Give your experience value. Whether it's in business or romance, life's easier when you focus on what you learned not how you learned it.

The priority with any mistake is you. You have to fix it. Disappointments are normal so keep your hopes intact. Don't feel sorry for yourself. Doubts will end your dream right there. No matter what, believe you'll get over it and succeed. Be kind to yourself. Consider the future. Respect the possibilities your choices create. When you miss something, recover your wits and go on. You didn't really miss it if you catch it in time. Be calm. Remember what you're doing and why. Brush away others' doubts but listen to them. Act responsibly. Never blame anyone. Responsibility deals with mistakes. Blame excuses them.

Blame undercuts teamwork. Individual efforts build into a team that goes in one direction. Your responsibility is to make that direction clear and have everyone understand that you need them working together. Teammates have to see each other as partners. When someone doesn't respect who they're working with, it compromises their dignity. People won't give 100% unless they're appreciated. Everyone has limits. At times they'll fail at their jobs. It affects everyone who's made your purpose their purpose. When something doesn't work, it's the team's responsibility to fix it. It's not about personalities. Momentum flows with the team's success. There's no individual blame. If someone doesn't fit, it's no one's fault. It's just a bad fit, like the wrong size shoe. It's your responsibility to find the right fit or adjust it to make it fit.

Choose people you trust. Without trust, everything's a gamble. Trust is essential for being sure things get done right. When you trust your team, they'll support each other. When a mistake is made, who did it doesn't matter. Recriminations are for people who forget they're on a team. When you or someone you depend on makes a mistake, no matter how serious, stabilize your emotions, find out what happened, fix the problem, and go forward. What's done is done. Mistakes are temporary conditions to be dealt with and left behind.

Paying Them Their Due

People need encouragement. You encourage them because it helps you. Your vision makes sense to them as something they can share. Whether people help you from love or just want another payday, their performance relates to the enthusiasm you instill in them. Your dreams lead you, your heart pushes you, even your fate compels you, but sometimes you have doubts. Nature's changes can throw you off your game. While you work at getting things right, you can only *hope* you'll achieve what you want. Sometimes your efforts are successful. Other times success comes by chance, like when you run into an old friend looking for just what you happen to have. You accept good results however they come. Without results, you only have hope. Fortunately, hope is manageable. You direct it through your belief that love will get you what you want.

Getting credit for your accomplishments is personal. If you measure your self-esteem by other people's opinions then praise matters. Your success becomes secondary to the recognition that honors you. That's fine. It's a character trait, not a fault. You can still be supportive, loving, fair, considerate, dependable, and all the other character qualities you respect. Or you may prefer your praise in private. Showy demonstrations may annoy you. You may shy away from the attention and find your approval in your own self-respect. That's another character trait. Different people need encouragement in different ways. Know the difference and encourage them in a way that respects them.

You remember your trials. You hope you'll handle things better if you ever get another chance. It's like watching the final out in the World Series when the championship is decided after a hard fought season. The winners run to each other and embrace with the biggest smiles of their lives. The season's mistakes are forgotten in the ecstasy of victory. The other team, though they've come through the season to play for the championship, bow their heads and feel like losers. What they wanted, the chance to be a World Series winner, may never come again. They nit-pick looking for the mistakes that cost them the season. Was it their play, a teammate's bad attitude, or bad breaks? No one's to blame. Everyone should be applauded for their effort. When the first pitch was thrown, one team was going to win and the other team lose. It's easy to be overwhelmed by the emotion in a big event. All you can do is feel it and get back to your purpose. Winning is in doing. A great victory is a rare bird but you're entitled to happiness every day of your life.

There are benefits to winning and costs to losing. Common sense tells you when someone might lie to win. You don't like it but you know it happens. People lie to avoid responsibility or claim someone else's accomplishment to enjoy benefits they don't deserve. With people you trust, who trust you, the truth, whatever it is, helps everyone. You don't know that with strangers. You give associates the benefit of the doubt until you trust them or not. You're not judging them. You're respecting yourself. Honesty is important to your purpose. Lies send you down a false trail. They waste your time. They cause injuries when safety measures are misrepresented and discord when people are blamed unfairly.

If someone can't do the job, it's not their fault. Your responsibility is to pick the right person for the job. If the job is beyond their ability, you made a mistake. Find someone else. Pay attention to their skills and attitude. You don't need a rocket scientist to fix the sink. You need someone who knows how to fix a sink. Trust your feelings. Don't ignore anything. You can do things right and still make a mistake when you're desperate or impatient. Relax. Give yourself time and you'll find good alternatives. You may think you can't live another day without air-conditioning and rush to pay exorbitant weekend repair rates when waiting a day could save you money. Life is the vehicle you create, so be realistic about your needs.

Once More...and Again

Trust your plan. Be enthusiastic with a clear goal each morning. You're not going to feel good every day. Regardless of your mood, keep your self-esteem intact. Trust the life God gave you even when things go wrong. Then, when life tells you "rest"...REST! Use your good sense to stay strong. Few can go 24/7 without breaking down. You don't want a health problem when you're making important decisions. Even when you feel strong, the stress of events can overwhelm you. Respect that your life needs maintenance and make that part of your plan.

You need psychic rest too. It's a fancy way of saying faith. Faith eliminates your fear of failure. You trust God's love will protect you. It's your belief in your security regardless of events. Through faith you accept your partnership with God. You open yourself to God's love and trust your comfort knowing you're supported.

A sincere effort is all you can do. You can't guarantee anything. You might think if you work harder, learn more, and build better relationships, you'll succeed. Common sense says that should work, that the answer to success is in doing more. You're a partner in civilization. You help direct it by sharing your love. Love connects you to everyone. Your belief in love's power focuses God's energy in your soul. Love is how you transform the world. Though people have different beliefs, reality can't avoid love. One way or another you know it whether you understand it or not. Through love, you're always on common ground. You know it because you understand why someone else loves their kids because you love your kids.

You control your beliefs. You can change them or remain steadfast. Sometimes you have that "Eureka!" moment in an instant realization when your mind unlocks to free you from some old habit, like when you realize online banking is easier than writing a check each month. Other times, your new understanding is on a mental level but your emotional belief is so ingrained it takes time to trust it.

Look for ways to succeed instead of focusing on your problems. It's the "Can do!" attitude epitomized in business, sports, and the military. Problems shouldn't be obstacles. They should be questions. Good habits repeat your intentions until you have the answer you want. It's the same as playing an instrument. You practice until you know enough to play it. Bad feelings aren't your enemy. Fears protect you. Respect them. But they shouldn't insulate you from life. Your first thought should be "Can you use it?" not "Could it hurt you?" Caution is wise when you control it. Don't let fearful habits replace your good sense.

Success begins with your plan. You maintain a plan in the same way you care for your health or your car. You're sensitive to it. You're sensitive to its changes. You're sensitive to what affects it. You avoid people with colds and drive around potholes. It's not a burden. It makes your life easier. No reasonable person should question your motives when they understand what you're doing. Your doubts concern them. You're the leader. Your attitude reflects the condition of your plan. You spread doubt in the same way you inspire success. Always express an attitude of achievement. Answer every question, "I can work this out." and you'll control your life.

Written In the Stars

There may be no logical reason why something goes well for you or why you can't move past some obstacle. "How did you get that great job?" "How did you get so sick?" Things happen and sometimes they happen to you. Many people don't believe in fate but I think it's real. You've heard, "You make your own luck." and "God helps those who help themselves." It makes sense. The more you focus on a situation, the better chance you have to succeed. It's obvious when you work harder you accomplish more. It's true, but it's just part of the picture. There's a mystical side to spirituality that provides specific challenges expressed as your fate. On your preordained path, you work within your fate.

Your soul is everything to you. You have abilities and responsibilities as a spiritual being. It's not religious. It's the reality of your spirituality. Whatever your beliefs, your soul knows its purpose. While religions have different perspectives on your soul, they all acknowledge your soul as an integral part of your choices. So here's the question you should ask, "What's my soul trying to do?" Once you realize that your soul's purpose inspires your conscious purpose, you'll find the answers you want.

Your fate guides your soul to develop certain characteristics in a certain way. So it provides appropriate opportunities to help you. It's your lesson plan. While it's common to everyone, it's not the same for everyone. People are short or tall with everyone else in-between. Fate's the same thing. For some, fate's a dominating force. There's little you can do to change it. Your success or hardship is unavoidable. Your life can contain both in varying degrees, but your course is set. Alternatively, you may find freedom in charting your own fate and enjoy the adventure in the unpredictability your life allows. Then your fate is to create new situations. It's ordained for you to set your own course. Whether you control 1% of your fate or 99%, either way, God supports you.

Fate exemplifies organization; purpose, starting points, paths, and goals. Everything in your life is organized. The earth and moon follow their daily circuits. Your heart beats its rhythm as your blood cycles through your body. Everything in your experience is a system where particles organize into atoms to become elements, then molecules, rocks, trees, animals, and through your creativity the house you live in and the car you drive…more systems. If nature is about organized systems, then why shouldn't your soul's experience be an organized system too?

If fate is a system, figure it out and live with it. Have peace of mind about it. Peace of mind comes from working within your limits. Ask yourself, "What comes easy and what comes hard?" If you're sincere and do everything you can, trust there's a benefit in the result even if it doesn't fit your plan. Fate's purpose is to educate you, not exalt or punish you. Sometimes it's best to give in. Other times it's best to hold on till your last breath. You never know what's over the next hill. Whatever it is, fate will give it to you. That's a guarantee. Trust your life. Trust fate. The universal balance is love, so fate is guided by love too.

Fate is positive. It's your balance between good times and bad. Trust your fate and you appreciate the transient nature of life, that whether you win or lose, you're in the right place to grow with it. Accepting fate is your trust in God's plan. You love your life by trusting its ebbs and flows. You can accept success without ignoring love and meet your problems without diminishing it. In spirit, you planned your fate so your life would be custom-fit to your soul's intentions.

The Test of Leadership

In the divine system of civilization there are people you're responsible to and others responsible to you. In a corporation, everyone in the accounting department answers to the Chief Financial Officer who answers to the President who answers to the Board of Directors who answers to the Shareholders, whether they own ten shares or ten million. Your economic situation has nothing to do with it. You follow the rules and respect the hierarchies. No one lives a solitary existence running naked through the woods living on berries and rainwater. You're responsible for making decisions that respect you and consider your community. Human beings depend on each other. In the ever-changing structure of civilization you must constantly reevaluate yourself. You want to be fair and still get what you want.

You dignify yourself when you respect others. When others have authority, like your boss or yoga teacher, you have to weigh that respect because there's a practical side. Will your boss hold back your promotion or give you a raise? Will your yoga teacher ridicule you or be patient with your progress? When a relationship is important but respect is lacking, you have to hope you can find a fair balance. It may be as simple as a word in passing but you have to step up and defend your dignity. Self-respect is your essential support. It's your acceptance of your basic value as a human being.

Set limits on the authority you give others. Protect your compromises and know when someone's stepping over the line. You set the rules for your self-respect. Regardless of a decision, you always expect to be respected. Common sense and communication maintain cooperation. Character comes from having personal values and respecting them regardless of the challenges. Bend and twist them but remember why you chose them. You chose them to help you deal with your challenges. You chose them because you thought they were the right way to live.

You do your best whether you're responsible for a decision or not. When others have authority, support the person in charge as you hope those you lead will support you. Even when others don't see it, you're always in charge of yourself. Answering authority, you do what's asked of you whether you're asked respectfully or not. Your leadership skills recognize your place in the hierarchy of responsibilities. You control it by choosing who you cede your authority to and the limits you'll accept. You can always go somewhere else. Leadership centers on you. You direct it or accept it. Just don't ignore it or you become a slave. That's why no one wants to be a zombie. Your free will is precious. Just ask someone in jail. You live in constant negotiations that require you to accommodate decisions even when you don't want to. Guiding yourself when others have authority is the real test of leadership.

Chapter 5
Making Things Right

Financial Limbo

Making money was always a mystery to me. I was desperate for it at times but I couldn't do anything about it. My fate is my life was given to me. I had jobs, did well, but I never advanced. I always had limits put on me. I had plans and good starts but I was never able to build on it. I was never promoted. I did okay because my financial life was a series of miracles. Whenever things got tight, something happened to drop money in my lap. There's comfort in miracles when you trust them. But it's often a stressful situation that summons them.

So driving a cab popped up and working for my father's printing business popped up which gave me a trade so I was able to get more jobs in printing which led me to sales which is what I do now. There were unexpected windfalls. But just as fast as God gave it to me, God would take it away. I've come to believe my financial life is directly managed by God. Car expenses and dental bills are favorites with God and the rare medical problem, need for a new roof, or a legal issue has from time to time knocked me on my financial butt. Lots of lessons. Lots of life to accept. I'm beginning to learn more about money including the opportunities it offers. I've learned it wasn't just me. Everyone in one way or the other is in the exact same situation. It's just when you have money, you can throw it at your problems and they go away.

Living by miracles is nerve-wracking but I'm getting the hang of it. The problem is, while I have no sense of control, I'm beginning to have more faith in life. I'm sincere in doing well and worry less when I don't. And then when I need it, a miracle happens.

Cycles & Trends

Your feelings give shape to your dreams. You project them physically, like when you think how good it would feel to have a cold drink and then you go get one. You sense that part of your identity. It develops from birth. Growing up you're inspired by your surroundings, from the mobile that hung over your crib to your choice of funeral arrangements. Certain things attract you. Before anyone knew you were musically talented or tall enough to be good at basketball, you made decisions. You explored life, gained experience, learned things, and chose one thing over another. From the very beginning you were self-reliant.

From a loved one you learned to take care of yourself, be safe, negotiate the social system, respect authority, and be a sensible, self-respecting person. Your reward, you hope, is a good life. Success shows you what works. Failure shows you what doesn't. The joke about life being "The School of Hard Knocks" describes the reality of life's unrelenting trials. It's unavoidable. No amount of money can save you from nature's misfortunes. There's no celebrity who doesn't have health problems, family concerns, financial issues, and doubts about their purpose and relation to God. Fame is just another path. Everyone is growing no matter who they are.

Energy needs a purpose. Your will gives it its purpose. Everything interacts with everything else, so when something changes everything changes. This happens continually and can be identified as trends. Trends are reliable guides. They're a history of events. They grant you the economy of looking at a few things to understand millions of opinions.

Trends recycle to reflect society's current interests. There are trends in fashion, economics, and politics. A fashion is more than what you wear. It's a social attitude. Sometimes the attitude is austere. Other times, it's expressive. In economics, sometimes you save more, other times you spend more. Trends follow social attitudes. In times of unrest, you put up your defenses for protection. In peaceful times, you let down your guard to free your spirit to explore its creativity. Personality types become more or less successful as they accommodate the trend, like what you see in today's attraction to TV reality shows. Trends follow success. Humanity's overwhelming trend is to grow. It means you can easily let your love create whatever you want within the trend.

Love guides trends. Problems occur when love is limited, like giving a privileged group benefits that exclude others. Fear for survival, real or imagined, is enough to make love a low priority. History shows there are cultures who try to rule their neighbors to take their resources or impose beliefs they feel are superior. It's common for nations to identify divergent beliefs and try to eliminate them. To them, dominating another's free will is justified. But it's never peace. It's faithlessness led by people who rationalize God's love to reflect their beliefs. You want a safe place to enjoy the fruits of your labor and love whomever you want. That's love's trend. But the growth of love for many cultures must be patient because it can take generations to mature.

A trend reflects the cycle of your maturity, your bond with society. Your goal is to explore your creative will as it's defined by your culture. That includes your friends, family, neighbors, job, religion, ethnicity, politics, interests, and your experience with relationships from snobbery to community service. It can change tomorrow or last you a lifetime. You can taste a bit of it or feast on it. Choose the mountains you want to climb. See if you like the view. Stay where you are or try something new. Your job is to love yourself and find happiness wherever you go. You love life's wildness because the love you identify with is everywhere. It's in the cities, in nature, even in the suburbs as you race to catch a sale at the mall. But without love, it's all a dead end.

You're always thinking about something.

Manage your thoughts. You depend on them. Nurture a positive attitude. Your thoughts will drift anywhere that solves their confusion. Junk thinking comes from immaturity. Self-importance, negative thinking, repeating resolved issues, a fascination with sports and trends, even giving up, your mind is always working. Take charge. When you can't think with a purpose, at least be positive. Daydream your hopes. Think about your successes to come. Deal with what's in front of you and don't over think it. If you find your answer in a negative image then your thinking is immature. It's common to follow gossip. Interest in someone else's life replaces interest in your own. If it's not some celebrity, it's a stranger or a friend. It's okay when it's balanced with self-respect. But you may find thinking about others easier and waste your time being fascinated by them instead of enjoying who you are and who you could be.

Your aspirations materialize in your thoughts. If you like, you can put your mind on hold and live your thoughts without attention. The trade-off is the opportunities you miss. Some people like an automatic transmission. Others like the control in a manual shift. It's your choice. But too much convenience can atrophy your creativity. Your mind needs purposeful activity because you can't shut it off. The electronic media is replacing drugs and socializing as convenient distractions. Through the Internet and TV you can gossip about people you don't even know. The danger is it can replace your originality with other people's stories. Electronic media is the blessing of our age, but you're the one who gives it value. Your mind needs intriguing questions or you'll bore yourself to death. Those are the questions you have to ask yourself.

Your most important memories come from your actions. Think about what you remember. Are you most proud when you talk about a movie you saw or if you visited the country in the movie? In participating, you have a deeper appreciation of your experience. You're not limited by the director's choices. You can explore whatever fascinates you about the place. Whether you like working on machines or cooking, you free your mind through your actions. You direct your thoughts away from your survival to absorb your mind in doing things where success or failure have no consequence. Call it a pastime or a hobby; it's important to you feeling free.

It can be any activity. The key is that it complements you. You like it. Read a book or write one. Build cars that go fast or drive ones that go fast. Be a chef or gourmet. A pastime appeals to you personally. Appreciate that you need practice. That's the point, learning more about it. There may be social stresses. You might shy away from something you like if you think others might judge you by it. Let self-love guide you. Participate. Enjoy yourself. Anyway, it'll take your mind off things.

The Pioneer Spirit

You can be a pioneer at any age. Keep your sense of self-reliance fresh. There are always things to discover. A pioneer isn't afraid of problems. They expect them. You look forward to the challenge. You look forward to the mysteries you'll solve. Your pioneer spirit loves the anticipation to enjoy what you don't even know exists. You can have that. You can be a pioneer.

Discover what you like. Be a pioneer in science and create new technologies. Be a pioneer explorer and travel to places little known to the world. Be a social pioneer and find new ways to create loving relationships. You're a born adventurer. You can't foresee how your life will turn out, but you don't need a fortune-teller. Much of what you

discover has been lost and rediscovered a thousand times. It's only new to you. You're meant to engage your life and master its mysteries. That's some trip.

Physics is the same everywhere. People are the same. Love is the same. You can relate to anything through love. Trust nature. Transfer your excitement into enthusiasm. Ask the right questions. "What's over there? Why did they do that? How can you use it? Who's that stranger?" Your instincts support you because you're designed to succeed.

You want comfort. You want to be warm when you're cold, dry when you're wet, rested when you're tired, fed when you're hungry, safe when you're doubtful, and enjoy good health and an interesting life. The more you can guarantee, the better you feel. Beyond that, all you can do is ask questions. You ask the world to make your life easier. The thing about answers is they don't always produce the results you want. So every moment you live is a pioneer experience. It may call for physical courage when nature resists you or emotional courage when you have challenges beyond your ability. You might need spiritual courage when all you can see is the hardship ahead. That's the life of a pioneer. You start a journey, but who knows where it'll take you? You start a friendship, but who knows how it'll end? You have a child, but only God knows how they'll turn out. Still, you can share the wonders you discover. That's the joy in being a pioneer.

Endless Ideas

You can't stop thinking so you might as well think about things you like. Nature's limits define your possibilities. You access your possibilities through your intentions. You have control over your intentions. They don't fly out of nowhere. Your world is happening now. Whatever you want, you build today. Whatever grievances you have are current only as long as you identify with them. If your memories comfort you, then keep them fresh. If they've outlived their usefulness, discard them with all the pain they caused you. Your confidence replaces the bitterness of your past mistakes. Free your thoughts to act from where you are, not from where you were.

Your questions are so natural you barely notice them. You may think you're on automatic but you're not. Your brain keeps your body alive, but your soul makes you a constantly thinking, creative human being. Your best thinking is done when you support your emotions. You may like the quiet of the beach at morning or prefer the rumbling of your motorcycle. Either way, it's only important that you find comfort in your thoughts.

How does one part of your mind guide it all? How do you characterize your happiness? Your senses are your situational awareness. Your emotions are your guide. Your thoughts are the paths to your goal. And your soul is your creative, free will. Your soul comes alive through your questions. If you pay attention, you can feel it. Everything is always on and the constant flow of information is hard to separate. Simplify it. Ask yourself, "Can you use this?" Ignore the rest. Your soul continuously feeds you directions targeting your goal. Your thoughts are your deliberate effort to free yourself from the confines of nature and build something better. A dog may know when to come out of the rain, but you can bring an umbrella.

You're constantly resetting your priorities. Circumstances have different values at different times. You compare the cost and benefit of what you're doing at the moment. You want the most from what you have because you'll always need more. Life's about consumption. Its limits force you to make value judgments. Love supports your choices beyond their material benefit. It's a challenge to trust love over results you can touch. But life's not about easy choices.

You change things through your ideas. Ideas create new values from existing ones. But your ideas need power. Your mind tires easily. Rest frees you from the distractions that can waste your energy. Sleep refreshes you. After struggling for an answer, once you've slept, often the answer becomes clear. At least, your courage returns with your energy. It may be a dangerous job that helps you to focus or the free expression you find in a classroom. Whatever it is, your mind has its best ideas when you're rested.

Today, Tomorrow, & Forever

You have an idea of your immediate future. My father used to say, "Tomorrow's another day." No matter what happened today, once you rested, you can start again tomorrow. Time is basically split into day and night. Most societies thrive in the daytime. But there are benefits to the night. It could be the unique nature in the solitude of the world at rest or the extra time to get things done. It's funny how in the dark of the early morning the people going out fishing for the day meet the hard partiers coming home late from the night before. Every day you work, tire, rest, recover, then work some more till it's time to rest again. It's a system. You just need to know where you fit in.

In today's 24/7 world, life moves fast. There's always something that needs your attention. Before all the technology you had time to catch your breath, but now international affairs have people getting up earlier and working later so they can stay ahead of any changes that affect them. It's important to be assertive in life, but don't worry about it. When you miss an opportunity, there's always another one right around the corner.

When the power goes out or a snowstorm blocks the roads, you accept the inconvenience and adjust your temperament while you wait for the lights to come back on or the roads to be cleared. There's nothing you can do about it. You excuse yourself because the energy you normally put towards your goals has nowhere to go. And the world doesn't crumble. It's rare that anything has to be done right away even when others get stressed about it. There's a saying in business, "There's never enough time to do it right, but always enough time to do it over." The pressure you put on yourself isn't real. It rarely exists outside your thoughts. Yes, it's important to fulfill your responsibilities. But you can do that without worrying. There's enough time to do whatever's necessary as long as you don't rush and make a mistake. What doesn't get done today, you'll do tomorrow. "Tomorrow's another day."

What do you want?

You decide your goals. Your achievements give your life meaning. It may be to write a popular play, raise healthy kids, or score the winning goal in front of 20,000 fans. You make it happen as best you can. Like hitting a golf ball, it's hand-eye coordination. Your mind's eye adjusts every part of you to hit the ball straight. Your mind instinctively guides your body without even thinking. If you miss, you correct it in your mind. You adjust your aim by changing your thoughts. Did you swing too fast? Was your shoulder in the wrong place? Your senses locate your goal. Your mind adjusts to reach it. You depend on the physics. You trust that things will behave a certain way. Just believe that your goals are possible.

Goals simplify your life. Clarity comes from all the decisions you *don't* have to make because they don't affect your goal. Only the thoughts you need matter. Your priorities crisscross every day. You finish one thing, start another, then the original one evolves and needs your attention again. Being comfortable with change is the trick to master. Life's always changing so you have to change with it. The beauty is your mind is flexible even if it means turning itself inside out. Who would have thought sex change operations would ever be so common?

Maturity is your opportunity to change. When your job and family were once your purpose, the time comes when you retire and your children start their own families. You have new freedoms, but now you need a new purpose. Or you might change relationships as old friends find new interests. No one's abandoning anyone. If you love each other, you'll support each other whatever direction you take. Everyone's purpose matters. You overcome inhibitions and explore new interests. You stop thinking about possibilities and enjoy new realities. A different career, moving to a new city, an interesting pastime, you come to accept yourself with less regard for how others see you. And when you're real, real people trust you.

Making Plans

Getting from point A to point B so you can eventually get to point C is the purpose of planning. It's that simple. It's the details that need your attention. You want everything to fit. When you know what to expect, you can guide it in the direction you want. It means you're not limited as long as you get to point B in good shape to move to point C. This is strategy, a series of conditions that advance you to the next position in your plan. Your actions, or tactics, should be appropriate to protect you as they help you achieve your goal. A goal is never finished. Regardless of your expectations, it grows. You want that growth to help you. While you appreciate your achievements, it's important to know where you'll go next. Your goal will always ask you for new directions.

If you don't know what you want, you have help. Learning positive thinking is great because it's all goal-directed. You'll definitely find something someone wrote about it from your point of view. It's a well-established concept, from Ben Franklin to Napoleon Hill. It shows you how to move forward from wherever you are, even if it's just regaining your balance after an emotional trauma. Desire guides you in the right direction. Essentially, you know what you want.

You're the only one who really does. Joy is knowing your purpose beyond simply wanting a loving spouse and lots of money. That's the same for everyone. That's nature's security. Self-love defines your joy. When you have a clear goal and reasonable values, you ride the horse instead of carrying it.

Your values evolve from your experience. Your priorities mature. You realize the money you invest in an education is a better value than having a new car when you're starting out. You can get that new car later. A brief romance shows its impermanence when compared to the loyalty of an old friend. It takes time to learn these things, sometimes a lifetime. Your teacher is your sincerity. It's a challenge to satisfy your opinion of yourself. Things are always changing. So when should you feel successful? Success is engaging your goals in good spirit. It's succeeding with your self-respect intact. Trust life wherever it takes you. Virgil wrote, "When everything humanly possible has been done, fortune favors the brave." Be satisfied knowing you did everything you could.

You live with others competing for the same things you are; business success, a parent's attention, even reservations at a trendy restaurant. Competition means having self-serving opinions. You have them. Others have them. People share their opinions, good and bad, well intentioned or not. It may be a friend or just someone you know. To them your life may be nothing more than mindless gossip. Your support for your purpose, that sense of self-worth, is your balance. When you hear an opinion, compare it to your plan. Is it something you can use? If not, appreciate where it came from, then ignore it.

Your plan is your security. When you're stressed out, sick, or tired, it brings you back to life. It guides you when you can't think straight. It re-energizes you. Trust it but be flexible. There are always opportunities. Keep it up-to-date. Resist being impatient. Give your plan a chance to work. Hold firm or scrap it and make a better plan. The essence of your plan is organization. It's a wish list. It's an excellent tool as long as your purpose is your focus, not your plan.

Don't get in my way.

Life's an obstacle you can't avoid. Survival is your mandate. You do it every day. From staying healthy to paying your bills, you live its reality. Failing at it can burden you materially and psychically, everything you need to be happy. Life seems so indifferent; a mystery defined by religion and philosophies even when you demand a better answer. Reality doesn't stop because you can't explain it. The question is, "Do you succeed by your efforts, God's will, or dumb luck?" Where's the sense in it all? How do you respect it? And, what's your creativity have to do with it?

Like it or not, life's trials feed your purpose. They force you to think creatively. They exercise your character to create your comfort. Even a life of ease has responsibilities. The question is how you use your resources. You set the values. Your patience, consideration, preparation, and courage help. It's a balancing act. Your goal can require years of dedication while your mood changes every day. It's like a lumberjack keeping their balance in a logrolling contest. Each day takes you forward and back, round and around, bobbing you up and down. And sometimes your only strength is your will to succeed.

You might like competition. But if competing isn't easy for you, learn how. Have clear values about what competing means to you. Competition in business is different from who wins the spelling bee. In a spelling bee your survival's not at stake. Competing doesn't mean winning at all costs. Few things beyond your liberty are worth that. You need limits, reasonable values appropriate to what you're competing for. Every day you meet someone who wants the same thing you do. It might be a job or the club championship. Whatever it is, if it has value, someone else will want it too. If you're creative, you can compete intensely, respect everyone, and still accept the result whoever wins. That's how you harmonize love with your achievements.

An obstacle can be an asset. It forces you to try new things. There's a soldier's saying, "When confronted by a wall blocking your path; you go over it, around it, under it, and if that doesn't work, blow it up, then find the person who built it and knock 'em in the head."

Obstacles appear to block you, but with clear goals they only change your course not your destination. Every path teaches you something. Don't be disheartened when life takes an unplanned turn. There's value in everything. Look for the benefit. As miserable as an illness is, recuperation can give you time to think and save you from a bad attitude's misplaced values. A frustrating job may inspire you to take a risk and start your own business. Your inability to get help may force you to take responsibility.

Let me see that.

You want to know as much as possible. You want insight into the heart of the matter. You want good advice. You want to know how to act and the price of a mistake. You want common sense to guide you. You want to be clear why a certain tactic is best. You want to be sure the details you know are accurate. You want to be sure you're not missing anything. You want to be sure you use your opportunities. You want to be sure of who you work with. You want to be aware of the rules that affect you. You want to be sure your resources are ready. You want to be sure what you're doing is legal. You don't have to like it. It's not a matter of convenience. It's life's reality. Absorb yourself in it. See it through your soul. Don't fool yourself. See it for what it is.

Knowledge comes from observation. You do it yourself or learn it from others. There are books on every aspect of humanity, from your local town history to global geography. Information on every social condition, from political science to how to grow hair, is available to help you demystify your human experience. This is the beauty of civilization. You don't have to know everything. Somewhere there's someone who's already been through it. You can have that knowledge by paying attention, reading about it, or getting experience. Knowledge is as light as a love song or as ponderous as the national census statistics. It just depends on what you want to know.

Whether your knowledge comes from years of study or the morning office gossip, the facts of life continually present themselves. It's your responsibility to tune in what helps you and tune out what doesn't.

76

Your mind absorbs and interprets the raw data. Then you decide what to believe about it. Is it reasonable or does it challenge your common sense? Look for other sources that prove it. You judge your information by how it serves you, even if it's just something to laugh about.

Art is about observation too. It relates different perspectives on your observations. Art expresses an idea through the artist's creative skill. The artist asks you to consider alternatives from their point of view. The artist aims questions at your psyche. They can take an accepted point of view or offer a radical alternative. They can express their point realistically or turn the details into abstract shapes to stimulate your thinking. They can take a mundane event to explain the surreal interaction between you and nature. The beauty is, unlike science, art has no limits. There's no way to measure your imagination. You can explore any possibility and make it real enough to grab your attention, at least as a work of art.

You don't need every detail. The perfect situation is knowing what you need when you need it. Your knowledge may not be perfect, but your wisdom will use whatever you have. Life shows you things. Some are subtle, like the unexpected sound of children laughing. If you're in a bad mood it might tell you there's hope, that somewhere someone's happy so it's possible for you too. If you're in a good mood, it might signal you're in touch with the joy that makes your life worthwhile. Be grateful. Pay attention to the odd event. What you learn is appropriate to your need. Whether it's from a friend's advice or a sign on a community bulletin board, how you use it is what gives it value.

Do you have enough?

You need assets. It's your time, money, friends, contacts, reputation, health, education, experience, wisdom, skills, talents, confidence, self-respect, personality, spirituality, sense of fair play, common sense, purpose, and love. Resources are assets you don't have, but you know you need them. Together they give you stability. That foundation lets you reach out and build the life you want.

You have a physical purpose and a spiritual purpose. Your assets and resources serve them both. Your life is yours to do with as you wish. You have a unique asset in the gift God gave you in free will. When you receive a gift, you know it's for you and not someone else. You might share it, but it's yours. It's such an intimate part of your nature you often don't see it for the miracle it is. Usually, the closest you come to it is when you decide what to wear in the morning.

Your creative free will is your greatest asset because you use it to change things. You can figure out new combinations that make your life better. Creativity is as simple as adjusting your pillow or as complex as inventing a computer chip. The point is, you have the ability. Some people are more creative than others or excel in certain areas. Some people's physical nature allows them to employ their creativity better. Not everyone is born with the body of a ballerina or the mind of a genius. You're a creative human being. Human beings don't come any other way. What helps you be more creative is understanding that your access to God's creative consciousness makes you able to solve anything you set your mind to.

Life is a material process so respect your material assets. When you use them up, you'll need more. Whether it's more money or more practice, your assets need maintenance. Your assets are as important as your desires if you want to make your dreams real. It could be as simple as a holiday card to let an old friend know you still care about them. Sometimes it's work to maintain your assets, like the attention you need going over your monthly bills. It could mean oiling your garden tools or respecting your health with regular check-ups at the doctor. Your assets are your support. You want to know they'll be there for you when you need them.

What are your spiritual resources? How do they serve your physical purpose? Most people believe in their spirituality. Even if you don't believe in God, you accept your responsibility to others. If you saw an injured person you'd stop to help them. Spirituality is mysterious so many people use religion to help them understand how to act responsibly. They sense their connection to God but they need to understand it better. People like religious rules as a way to make sense of their responsibilities. But beliefs are personal. It's common for people of the same religion to have different interpretations of the same belief while others find bending their belief not so bad as long as there's a worthwhile benefit.

All souls have the same purpose, to live and dream about the future. It's how you work out the details that makes your experience unique. Love brings everything together. Though the details may change, survival is the same for everyone. Creativity is the same. Love is the same. Your purpose is to live, love, and create. Your life is the stage where love's adventure meets God's questions. Nothing is permanent. You leave everything behind when you die. A hundred years from now, it's likely no one will know you were even here. Except in rare cases, even the most famous of their time are forgotten. Your life is happening now. You appreciate what your predecessors achieved, but you live the present on your own. This is where *your* achievements are made. Your eternity is today.

If your soul's purpose is to ask questions, then life makes sense. You can see it as your connection to God, your inner consciousness, or your subconscious self, but the premise is you know more than you think you do. It means you have insights you can use. It's your ability to enquire of yourself at a higher level. Meditation, contemplation, intuition, epiphanies, and prayers are the paths to your insight. Be open to it and you'll discover answers you didn't know you knew.

Take what's yours.

Even when you know what you want, life's a challenge. You know what you'd like to happen, but you don't know the result till you live it. Life's predictable in your plan. In practice, it's a hope. Traffic can delay you regardless of your need to be on time to an appointment. When traffic's backed-up, do you stay on the highway or take a side road? There's no way to be sure which is faster. If you hear a traffic report, is it current or a half hour old? Every moment throws another decision at you. Should you call now or later? Does your shirt match your pants? These seem like trivial questions but you still have to answer them. It's your priorities in simple decisions that show who you are.

Whatever your plan, the future is unknown. Your adventure is in how you engage the unknown. The usual image is an explorer venturing deep into some unknown region or testing their endurance against some extreme physical challenge. As an explorer you crave the experience. You even compete for the opportunity. It can be physical, mental, or emotional, like your choice to be a performer or join an elite military unit. Testing the limits is how you explore life. Your adventure doesn't exist in some far-off place or by taking unnecessary risks. Even a race car driver wears a helmet. Your adventure is your choice to use your opportunities despite the uncertainties.

Your goals may predict your adventure but they're not the reason for it. Your goals have limits. Your adventure has no limits. You can change a goal. It may be important to your plan but it doesn't define your adventure. Your goals are important to your happiness but they're unimportant to where your adventure takes you. The question is, "What will you do when you get there?" Go beyond the image and embrace the value in your adventure, the things you'll do and the people you'll meet. You'll find your expectations, but you'll find surprises too. If you had your choice, everything you did would be successful. Life's not like that. Few roads are that easy because you wouldn't have as many questions.

"Life's a journey." It's an old saying often repeated because it's true. Your accomplishments may not reach the heights of acclaim. Regardless of your achievements, your victories may not affect another soul. Even the most accomplished have problems where their achievements have little effect on their personal lives. In a basic way, your life is the same.

Who isn't awed by the story of a single mother working two jobs, raising three kids, and sending them all to college? You have to make sacrifices to get what you want. You have to handle your problems and stay focused on your goals. Things don't always work out. You may face forces beyond your control. Common sense shows you that many of your concerns have been handled successfully by others so you know it's possible. No self-respecting adventurer rushes into the unknown. Consider your situation. Success is in your efforts to push past your limits and find a way to go forward.

Don't let anyone rain on your parade. There can be conflicts in different points of view. Learn to cooperate. This is the hard part of adventuring. You have to respond to the alternatives other people want. You want to be fair and open. It may be a new idea to you. Now you have to evaluate it and consider the responsibilities, all while the other person is arguing their point. These are the moment-to-moment decisions that define your life. The success of your adventure lies in supporting your values. Temporary results matter less than you think.

Mi Familia

Your world revolves around your personality. You have a style all your own. You have an identity in your likes and dislikes. You express your personality in your demeanor and relationships. You share your adventures and understand them in others. Your support will always be where people love you for who you are.

In a nuclear family, the intimate connection is your support. Parents raise their children, siblings help each other, and children grow up to support their parents. These are the basics of the ideal family where everyone creates opportunities for the others. The family is humanity's lifecycle. When it's successful, support grows through aunts and uncles, in-laws, and everybody's friends. But with a family, you're stuck with the personalities you get. You might not like them all. Still, your history bonds you together so, at least, the opportunity is there.

When you're dealing with children, you have a responsibility to society to make sure your children are cared for. This repeats itself with sick or elderly family members who, like small children, can't take care of themselves. It's like a three car pile-up. Your responsibility to a needy family member crashes into the time and financial resources you need to support them. That crashes into your responsibilities to live a happy life for yourself and the others in your life while your attention goes to help the loved one who's needy. This forces you into uncomfortable compromises. Some people sacrifice themselves. Others sacrifice the loved one. Money helps. Friends help. Religious and social organizations help. The government helps. Modern medicine can keep a sick person alive long after their quality of life is done. Where that balances with your desire for a life of your own is the question.

Your work relationships mirror the family system where everyone tries to help each other as they try to succeed themselves. You respect your colleagues whether you like them or not. You have the same conflicts anywhere people have an opinion. It's just politics. Whenever you negotiate with others, *which is always*, politics are involved. Other people's decisions affect you. At home, work, or whenever you have an opinion, it's important to be considerate, respect yourself, and find the compromises that can satisfy everyone's position.

Even the best solution can burden someone in the family, so that means everyone. Everyone needs attention. The family's resources help everyone. It's hard to favor one member over another. You need all your love, emotional strength, and common sense to support a shared outcome you know won't satisfy everyone. There may not be enough money to send all the kids to college. An elderly family member's illness may take the resources set aside to buy a teen family member their first car. All you can do is trust your sincerity, make your choices, forgive your mistakes, and let God decide the result.

The Social Orbit

Your life is cyclical; an endless series of beginnings, advances, obstacles, retreats, adjustments, accomplishments, and then new beginnings. It encompasses everything you are physically and spiritually. Only nature limits you. Whether it's a physical condition or social responsibility, your challenge is to control the flow of life's energy. Sometimes it's best to let things happen if they move where you want to go. But it's never exact. Always know where it's taking you. Sometimes you'll decide it's better to nudge it in a new direction. Other times, you'll seize control to prevent a problem or exploit an opportunity. So, be aware. As hard as it is, your awareness and confidence are your ability to deal with the endless pattern of changes that make your life what it is.

"I should have stayed in bed today." How many times did you wake up and dread the ringing phone would bring you news of some new disaster? On the upside, you can have one of those days when miracles surprise you with news of unexpected successes. Then someone tells you, "You should buy a lottery ticket. It's your lucky day." What makes your luck? How can an astrologer see the position of the planets and predict what kind of day you're going to have just because you were born at a certain time? They're not guessing. They're using nature's patterns. They make assumptions they interpret intuitively to make predictions. I find horoscopes accurate in a broad sense, not specific as much as they're an inclination of the day's energy. To avoid too many opinions I pick one I like. I'm not saying you should believe in them but it's in the news every day so a lot of people agree.

Consider the energy of the day. Not all days are the same. "How was your day today, dear?" The personality of your day is never certain. Some days you feel rushed with no outward signs of pressure. Other days you feel comfortable, at peace with just being alive. Some days you're in a good mood. Other days you're in a bad mood. Some days the rain feels dreary. Other days the rain feels like a blanket of protection. Both for no discernible reason. Could it be something affecting everyone? Civilization moves to a common beat. The world has its energy too, times of bounty and times of fear. That energy can shift society's structure into new creations, be it destructive wars or peace and trade. You're part of it. You're affected by the world's energy every day.

Do you curse it or give thanks? You can't control universal energy by overpowering it. You work with it by controlling your attitude. Trust it as part of nature. It's like a snowstorm blocking the road making it hard to pass. It's a lot of work shoveling snow, but it's fun when you roll around in it making snow angels. "Every cloud has a silver lining." is the wisdom that problems shouldn't be feared. Hardships can be opportunities. Many problems don't end by anything you do but by their natural cycles completing themselves, like when a flooding river crests and finally recedes within its banks. Be successful by using your creativity to make the best of your environment. Nature accepts you as part of it and will respond positively to your positive efforts.

You have options. You can still control your experience. You can adjust your plan to accommodate the energy as simply as you'd cancel a day at the beach if it's raining or take a day off and go to the park on a beautiful day. You don't control the energy. You control your responsibilities within the energy. You can avoid conflicts and take risks that succeed when you accept universal energy exists. Adjusting to it is the challenge.

So Sad

You don't always succeed so moving past your disappointments is essential to being happy. A disappointment can be as trivial as a scuffed shoe or as serious as a car accident. It can marginally disrupt your routine, like a flat tire, or be life changing, like waking up with a pain that turns out to be a serious health problem. It's funny how car repairs are high on the list of unexpected disappointments. You're surprised that while you go about your normal maintenance, you actually find something wrong, expensive to fix, and impossible to ignore. You pay whatever it costs, not to achieve something new, but just to get back to where you were. That's the nature of disappointments. They're unavoidable problems. Sometimes you can fix them. Sometimes you can't. Adjusting positively to disappointments is how you create your faith.

Those are your day-to-day disappointments. The big disappointment is when your plan fails despite your best efforts. Then your sincerity is challenged. You can pray, work hard, invest everything you have, but still your plan doesn't work. You thought you could do it. You accepted the responsibility. Many eastern pioneers in America's early history set out for California only to break down along the way where they settled and built successful lives for themselves. They revised their plan to take advantage of their circumstances. Their original effort was successful in the sense it created opportunities they wouldn't have had if they hadn't begun their journey. Dealing positively with disappointments is important because your success may be somewhere you hadn't expected.

A disappointment sends you in a new direction. It's not a "Stop" sign. It's a "Turn Here" sign. It's not an option. It's an order. It tells you something has to change for you to move forward. Expect reasonable problems. When they come, you can have the answer ready. Once you've exhausted your emotional pain, you can fix the problem. Don't identify with your disappointments. Don't ignore your feelings but don't energize them beyond their worth. Something you didn't want happened. That's all. Continue from where you are. You don't want a disappointment to be a burden. Learn from it, release it, then move on.

Disappointment in others is common. It could be your kids' grades, higher prices at the gas pump, or an inconsiderate driver who cuts you off on the highway. You share the world with others so everything is a negotiation. Whenever people meet, there's a need to satisfy common interests. You choose your priorities. They choose theirs. Compromise makes the agreement. It happens in every social situation and between nations where cultural differences clash or harmonize depending on their leaders' ability. When a disagreement denies you what you want, you're disappointed. Your disappointment needs a fair balance to fix it. But how do you decide the value of unequal issues? To one side it may be more important how fast the question gets solved while the other side is more interested in how much money they make. A good compromise trusts fairness. You're born with the tools that make it work. You have love, common sense, and through your creativity the ability to find alternatives that satisfy everyone. Whether everyone agrees is up to them.

The danger in disappointment is self-loathing. It's hard not to take things personally. Guard yourself against self-pity, resentments, and rationalizations. Those thoughts feed your emotional pain. Their presence identifies your lack of control. When a disappointment happens, stay focused on your purpose. Your emotions react normally to disappointments. This happens all day with the thousands of reactions you have to your changing environment. It's no reason to blame yourself. Keep in mind what's right for you.

Making things right takes time. Patience is your sanctuary away from emotional pain. Disappointments can be frightening. They force you out of your comfort zone. Their message is that you're ready to create a new comfort zone that can accommodate them.

Whatever it takes. Wherever it takes you.

You need courage if you want anything. Whether it's a raise or a date, life has opportunities you'll miss without courage. Everyone loves to say they know someone in the military, a cop, someone who started a business, or anyone worth admiring for taking a chance. You feel safer thinking there's someone with courage who'd help you in a tough situation. What supports you most is knowing you're the brave person. Courage is your emotional strength. Courage is your decision to stand up for what you want. Your courage is in facing the uncertainties in your responsibilities, sometimes as simple as calling someone you don't know and asking them for help.

Courage comes with confidence. Your fears are a warning. Courage helps you trust the wisdom in your fears and calm yourself enough to act sensibly. It's the old adage about "fight or flight." There are pros and cons. You have to come to terms with yourself and decide which is best under the circumstances. History has heroic stories of smaller armies defeating larger ones. And no general ever wants to retreat but they'll do it when that awful choice is their best choice. Courageous choices don't guarantee success other than the certainty that you made a sincere choice when you had to.

Some people are naturally courageous in the same way some people are good at sports. For most, experience teaches you courage. If you respect the value in courage, you can train yourself to make courage part of your character. Everyone resists what's uncomfortable. The question is, "Will you suffer the resistance and accept being blocked or take action in the face of uncertainty and overcome it?" If you weigh the cost of action and its possible return against the expense of inaction and the possible result, if there's no real danger then you'll never know if you'll be successful until you try.

Fearlessness is different. Fearlessness is defenselessness in the sense that defenses aren't needed because you're going to do what you have to regardless of the situation. You respect your environment. Then you move forward toward your goal. No thought can stop you. Like Admiral Farragut's famous command at the battle of Mobile Bay when he was told there were torpedoes in his path, "Damn the torpedoes! Full speed ahead!" It's not recklessness. It's a conscious approach to achievement that's clear on its purpose, accepts the costs, but doesn't accept fear as part of your decision.

Your courage grows with your maturity. Surviving life's trials shows you the difference between what's dangerous and what only seems dangerous. The fears you conquer add to your confidence. You'll know what to do the next time you meet them. That gives you power. Even the most worrisome difficulties are manageable once you do them a few times. What once seemed terrifying, you learn is another of life's patterns. Problems may seem complex, but your courage gives you the ability to deal with everything in a sensible way.

Do you know who I am?

Fame is good when it's appropriate. It can help you get what you want. It means respect. When people respect you, they'll listen to you. They'll believe what you have to say. Everything you do reinforces your reputation. When you deal with people who don't know you, a good reputation is enough for them to trust you. It's a useful tool in a skeptical world. It dispels doubts where distrust in strangers is your natural defense.

Fame and celebrity are different. Celebrity is something the media uses to personalize their stories. Celebrity is about interesting people who symbolize cultural trends. They're entertaining. Fame might be limited to a small group like when a computer genius is famous among technology experts but unknown to the public. Particular fame and popular celebrity often overlap as people rise to the top in their field and the public learns about their achievements. People know you for your achievements even if it's only getting on TV or being photographed with a famous person you don't really know. It's fun to associate with role models and share their achievement. It's a great opportunity to enjoy a favorable opinion.

Can you cultivate fame as a resource? Absolutely. That's what advertising does. That's what publicity does. It uses the media to get your message to as many people as possible. Your message is, as they say in advertising, "a call to action." "Dear public, please do this. Buy this. Support this." It's the reason for celebrity endorsements. The message piggybacks on the celebrity's renown so the public trusts it. The messages are tailored to a particular audience in words they can trust. It's soft and gentle for young mothers buying laundry soap or aggressive with blaring music for selling fast cars to young adults. The goal is simple. To have the audience respond, "Yes. I'll do that!" And you do the same thing when you advertise your local charity on a t-shirt.

Famous or infamous, your reputation is what people expect from you. Whether it matters to you or not doesn't concern them. What matters is their awareness of the probable conditions of their relationship with you. People want to be confident that they'll benefit in their relationship so give them a good reason to trust you. Care about them. They'll remember you well and share their opinion with others. In a society of strangers, a good reputation helps when there's nothing else to depend on. A good word from a trusted friend is more reliable than the best sales pitch.

Do I have to draw you a picture?

"Use your common sense." Everyone knows that. Be practical. Be logical. Respect your instincts. Respect what you were taught, the same things you teach your kids. It's been drilled into you so many times it's second nature to say, "If your friend jumped off a cliff, would you jump too?" You wouldn't. You know better. You know what hurts. You know what feels good. You know when people are happy. You know when they're sad. You know the values people prize. You know what they hate. You even know the gray areas when people say, "Life isn't always black and white." Then, there's your creative potential, the same potential for change everyone has. How well you use it takes common sense.

Common sense will usually give you the best result. It avoids dangers and exploits opportunities. It's your basic instinct to feel good, be safe, and have what you want. Common sense evolves through your experience but grows differently than your intellect. It's less analytical. It relies on your soul's feeling, "Is it right?" It's not mental acuity. It's your soul's awareness of what's good for it.

You reap its benefits without even noticing. Behind the scenes, it seeks the value in your problems. It's only the most confusing problems that need your analysis. Confusion can cause hopelessness and bury your good sense in doubts. Then bad ideas gain traction as the balance in your common sense weakens and any solution seems attractive. Common sense is the cure for bad judgment. When your alternatives are unpleasant, trust your common sense to mitigate your desperation and lay the groundwork for a successful solution.

Common sense is your intuitive respect for your feelings. It attaches no circumstance other than what's best for you. Particulars and personalities don't matter. If you want to question a sixth sense beyond your traditional senses, it should be your common sense. Psychic awareness is more like a seventh sense, a connecting awareness between your physical and spiritual worlds. Common sense is the bridge between your mind and sub-conscious. When you make an effort to increase your understanding, you activate your common sense.

The best thing is you're born with it. Your common sense supports your love for the world and everything in it. It makes sense of the fairness in every situation and what's right to expect. It can predict the outcome if one path or another is chosen. It would support you if you woke up alone in the desert and didn't know where you were. All you have to do is trust it.

What's your plan?

It's impossible to know everything. But before you know anything, you need to know what you want. You know where you are. You have an idea where you want to be. So how do you create a path to get there? You need a plan.

Your plan is a conscious effort to guide yourself. It's your thoughts organized into a sequence of events aimed at your achievement. It's your expectation of problems and opportunities. It can end in your achievement or develop into a new plan. However you do it, you direct it. So write it down. Remove the burden on your memory and keep your thinking fresh. Add what improves it. Eliminate the clutter. Your plan grows with your evolving values because it's always controlled by you.

You may not realize how much plans are part of your life. How many times have you said, "What's your plan for the weekend?" "Do you plan on getting married?" "Do you have a retirement plan?" You're really saying, "Have you considered how you're going to get what you want tomorrow by taking certain steps today? Do you have a plan?" You should. The time you spend planning is an investment in yourself. Just knowing it is the first step.

You learned about planning early in life. Remember when you had time off from school for "Teacher's Planning Day." Who cared what it meant. It was a day off from school. But somewhere there were teachers meeting on the best way to teach the community's children. It was important. After taking time for consideration and decision-making they could get back to the job of teaching and rely on their plan to take them through the school year. If the plan had problems, they'd fix them at the next planning session. Even with the best intentions a plan needs flexibility. Everyday situations must be addressed even when they haven't been considered. Misunderstandings need to be clarified. New ideas need testing. It's important to a school system in the same way it's important to you. It's your path to success.

Encourage feedback. You may not agree with it but it's smart to consider sincere opinions. You may find a better way of doing things. Advice doesn't change your plan. How you include it is up to you. Your plan may include being part of someone else's plan, like an employee. A business has an identity too. It has a plan. You decide if you want to be part of that plan. You decide if your responsibilities to it are worth the benefits to your own plan.

Contracts are plans. In a lease or any business agreement, clause after clause list the conditions of the contract, its plan. There are health plans to insure you have enough money to pay your medical bills, wills to direct the distribution of your assets after you die, and living wills to direct others what to do if you're ever incapacitated. Plans touch every part of your life. Plans are as simple as a vacation schedule or as complex as the master plan for a city. From outlining a grade school book report to planning your wedding, you use plans. But you don't need an expert to make a good plan. You need common sense, a goal, reasonable values, a good sense of timing, and a pen...or, at least, a smartphone with a good calendar app.

Prepare now.

The purpose of your plan is preparation. Preparation is your understanding of possible conditions and being ready to deal with them. Preparation is about the future, whether it's getting an education or putting gas in your car to be sure you have enough for the day.

The opposite is being unprepared. These aren't equal opposites. While preparation can give you an opportunity to succeed, a lack of preparation doesn't always leave you flat. It can move you backwards. Missed opportunities can make the road longer, but not being prepared *for something you should have known about* can cost you everything. Just ask someone who's been through a natural disaster. You can avoid a lot of hardship when you're prepared.

But how do you prepare for the unknown? You use common sense. You know what to expect when you pay attention. The right question should lead you to the right answer. You know that when one thing changes everything can change. You hear people say, "I should have bought that land twenty years ago. It was cheap then. Now it's worth a fortune. I could have been rich." It just means that person wants to be rich. If they were serious, they would look forward twenty years and buy some land today. It just needs commitment. Preparation is your commitment.

Life is uncertain so prepare for the likelihood something will happen. The future may not be as you planned but some of those things might happen. It's a value judgment. Preparation for tomorrow is a trade-off against what you need today. An effective plan keeps up with changes. While a million things you don't know can happen, you always know the result you want.

Preparation depends on what you need. Will others be competing for the same supplies you want when a hurricane's coming? Do you have the right skills for your dream job when opportunity knocks? Preparation is an advantage in competition. The preliminaries are already done. You're ready to take action. You can't prepare for everything. There's too much to consider. But you can build your confidence, educate yourself, have some money ready, and understand the future is sensible even when it's unpredictable.

I had it just right.

Change happens. Anticipate it when you can. You initiate it or it surprises you, so expect all life's possibilities. See beyond them. Good or bad, there's opportunity in everything. Think positively. Don't suffer a change without somehow growing through it. Respect yourself. You create your life in the way you adjust to change.

Change doesn't mean something new happens. Everything's been happening forever. It's just new to you at the moment. It means your change has a history. In the human experience, everything's been done every way possible. There are books on everything from every point of view. The phone book is full of services for any dilemma. It's like buying your first home. There's a big change between your blissful dream of home ownership and the reality of maintaining it.

Controlling change starts by knowing you have help. You don't have to know everything. Society means you help others and they help you. You just want it to be fair. Most people like helping others. They just want to be respected.

Change means something's happening. If you planned for it, you can guide it. Without a plan, you still want what's best for you but now you have to scramble to figure out what you need. You can prepare for anything. You can buy insurance, eat well, get enough rest, educate yourself, build friendships, have confidence, and save money. These form the foundation for your life no matter what happens.

Your life changes from moment to moment. The particulars don't matter. Having the resources to deal with them matters.

Times change. What was once a successful trend can turn stale as new ideas invigorate a culture. You can go with what's new, like today's social networking, or retire to the well-worn paths you've known for a lifetime. After a while, it's all one big ball of life with change just something normal to expect. Every generation has its new hairstyle. As different as science fiction makes the future seem, people will always have their likes and fears. People stay the same. Only the technology changes. They used to call them "flicks." Today we go to the "movies." Sometimes only the name changes.

Specific changes are unpredictable. You'll always find something you didn't expect. Life's an adventure. Most of the time it's exciting to move somewhere new, as long as it's not to prison. You'll always need life's basics wherever you go. Even though the people are different, human relations are the same. Even with foreign values, life's the same everywhere. People eat, sleep, raise their kids, and create. The sexes mingle. People laugh, cry, work, and play. They express themselves through the same creativity God gave everyone. People love each other. No matter where you are, you can relate to anyone through love. That never changes.

Fit as a Fiddle

How can you feel energetic every day? How do you support your vitality on those long Thursday afternoons? As you grow older, you slow down. You don't have the strength you had in your twenties. Health problems come up, the result of bad habits or a lack of awareness about the long-term effects of dangerous environments, overwork, or a careless diet. Your bones move around and your body weight changes. Normal stuff. Your human machine wears down. Your body isn't designed to last forever. Look at someone 100 years old. They're not going to make it to 200. Your lifetime is limited. So where do you find the energy to enjoy your life at any age? Do you have a choice?

You want to feel good. You want to feel strong. That comes naturally, but it's easy to lose it. Aging and illness can take your strength. From your energetic youth, you peak and then decline. Your maturity and experience compensate. Wisdom replaces your physical strength. You work around your weaknesses. But you can prepare for your body's future today. Respect your health, not just when you lose it. It's the proverbial, "You don't miss the water till the well runs dry." It's not about having good health insurance. Good health is your insurance. Protect it. Respect your body like it was a fine antique. *Take care of it.*

Good health is a social responsibility. You don't have to wear a surgeon's mask everywhere you go, but it's a good idea to wash your hands and respect others who may be affected by your hygiene. You'd take a day off from work if you had a bad cold so no one else would catch it. If you need help because you have a serious ailment, the community lets you get a handicapped parking permit so you don't have to walk so far. The good sense in good health is evident on every shelf at the drugstore.

So, get enough sleep. Try not to worry. Trust your faith. Feed your psyche positive thoughts. Exercise. Participate. Communicate. Have goals. Get advice. Reduce your stress. Control your emotions. Control your drinking. Explore life. Be interested. Be kind. And love yourself.

Make yourself strong. Live your adventure but be sensible about it. Respect the opportunities your good health gives you. Be a step ahead. Create opportunities for your body to strengthen itself. Your well-being is the best preparation for any problem. Your body renews itself. Whatever help you give it is appreciated.

Your health is about as intimate as you can get. It's your physical state of being…and your freedom. You're keenly aware of it even as minor as a hangnail. It can make you weak in the knees just having a doctor give you bad news about your health. Your good fortune is the cumulative experience of everyone who's ever valued their health. Talk about an ailment and it's a safe bet you'll get an opinion and a story. There's no lack of information. It's up to you to use it.

Hey, Old-Timer!

You mellow with age. Life becomes less frightening. What once seemed essential, experience shows you didn't matter that much. You learned that no matter how careful you are, life can still jump up and bite you in the butt. So be sincere and do your best. Most things will fall your way. If they don't, you do something else. You work within life's limits. Time is your teacher. What once seemed confusing eventually becomes second nature.

Your maturity blossoms in how you deal with people's opinions. You get tired worrying about what someone might think if you do this or don't do that. You do things because you want to and see no harm. You don't always have to put on your make-up or shave to go out. The older you get, those things are less important than being a loving human being. Your good looks as a teenager won't help you when having a good friend is what you need as an adult.

Your values mature. You learn what's important. You want to be healthy. You want to be safe. You want to be confident. You want to wake up with a purpose. You want your soul to express its creativity. Your comfort is in understanding there are many things you worry about that really don't matter. And what does matter, you can have any time you want.

You deal with the big problems. The small problems you learn not to mind. A passing bad feeling isn't worth the time. Like getting stuck in traffic or dealing with a foolish clerk, all you can do is be patient. That's where your peace of mind comes from. The rain won't stop because you hate it. If you can't accept nature, you're going to be miserable. You can't control nature. You can only control your attitude toward it.

You can achieve anything over time. Time creates opportunities for change. Time turns your good sense into good habits. With time, your efforts grow into the accomplishments you planned. Maturity teaches you that nothing's a rush so don't pressure yourself needlessly. Disappointments are aggravating. You control them by taking time to fix them.

Be clear on what you need. Your comfort is in satisfying your needs. But don't rationalize your compromises if the balance doesn't fit. That's the confusing question. Is your comfort in your dream or in understanding what you want and accepting it when you have it? Your common sense and self-respect show you what's important. They rely on your soul where your opinion is always perfect.

Time teaches you gratitude. Gratitude is the connection between God and your humanity. When you receive gratitude, it's satisfying to know someone respects you for caring about them. Their gratitude completes the bond you share in God's love. People help you. They console or inspire you, or lend you a ladder. Your gratitude acknowledges them so their love can grow too.

M-O-N-E-Y

Money is a merry-go-round. You're merry when you have enough to live the way you want. So you plan for it. You work at it. And you grow up. When once you wanted stylish clothes and a fancy car, now you save money for a house and a college fund for your kids. But conditions change. You can work twenty years for a company and come in one day to find the business closed. Bills and no income is a hard pill to swallow. What do you do? *All you can.* If things that were good can turn bad, it means bad times can turn good again.

"Save some money for a rainy day." You hear that all the time. Your life thrives on money. As long as you have money your expenses don't matter. You pay them. The problem is when the spigot turns off and you still have bills. You can walk away from an expensive dinner but you can't avoid eating. You can't avoid your contracts. Your obligation to a mortgage or car payment is a continuing expense. If the asset can be sold, you can get some value and reduce your expenses. Even at a loss, you're on firmer ground to start again. Sometimes a contract can be renegotiated to give you more time to improve your finances. Whatever the circumstances, you're still responsible for your bills. Money matters.

Money's always on your mind. Money's on everyone's mind. Kids want money for jeans. Teenagers want money for gas. College costs money. A house and a family cost money. A vacation. Dental bills.

Car maintenance. A new air conditioner. A new roof. Surgery. A divorce. Taxes. Retirement. These aren't once in a lifetime bills. And they can come in waves. Life is expensive even for penny-pinchers. But the cost of living is somewhat fair or no one could afford it. It's always possible to afford your life. Affording a specific lifestyle is different. The most economical way to manage your money is knowing what you want. Only pay for what you want.

Regardless of the values foisted on us by modern marketers, you can be satisfied when you know what you want. Good quality is still available at reasonable prices. The value in an expensive dinner, while it may be a good meal, is often the pleasure you get bragging about it. Status is a fun game, but it's a game. The fault with status is the belief that a person is superior because they can afford to waste their money. You can certainly spend more than reasonable to give someone a special experience. Then your expense has value. It's the financial value in love, the same as in a charity. Your saving grace is your creativity is the perfect substitute for money and it has no limits.

Sometimes you're financially on top. Other times you go begging. Homeless people beg. Big corporations beg. Some people win the lottery. Others are born with so much talent the world throws money at them. You probably live somewhere in-between with the rest of us, with highs and lows that come and go. There's plenty of advice on how to make money. "Get-rich-quick" schemes are as old as civilization even if they're new to you. Sometimes they work. Most are a wasted investment. If they were that successful everyone would do it. People follow success. History teaches that the path to success is to get an education, work hard, build your relationships, seek opportunities, have courage, and don't give up. It's no guarantee. It's just all you can do.

Protect yourself at all times.

Insurance is a good defense for unplanned expenses. Even with reasonable care, problems arise with costs you didn't expect. You pay for insurance to reduce the financial strain of unexpected expenses from an accident, illness, or any kind of loss. You pay the insurance company in advance. If the problem occurs, the insurance company pays you what you agreed to cover the loss. Insurance is your belief that it's possible to control the unknown when the future is important to you.

Insurance prearranges your resources. It's usually money but it can be anything. Having your car serviced before a long trip insures that your car is dependable. Bringing an umbrella on a sunny day is your insurance that you won't get wet when you know it might rain that afternoon. Taking extra cash on vacation, *just in case,* is your insurance you'll have a good time despite the possibility you might spend too much. It's an expense, but do you need it? How much will you need? What other insurance do you have? Yes, it's work planning for the unknown. But it makes sense to have extra batteries when the lights go out.

The biggest problem with insurance is complacency. If you buy insurance and think it's over, think again. Policies change. Rates go up. Coverage is reduced. So review your insurance regularly. The time you spend going over your policies is your assurance that you'll have the best coverage at the best price. Change companies when you find a better deal. It's a competitive business. It takes some effort but you can work through it easily with an insurance broker. When you find a better fit, it's easy to change. Fill out a form, write a check, and send a cancellation note to your old company. If the language in a policy is confusing, ask about it. Your policy is a contract. Don't expect the professionals to know everything. Talk to friends. Check industry associations. There's help available. Be an alert consumer and keep your insurance fresh.

Insurance should be part of every plan you make. Double-checking your work is insurance that you didn't make a mistake. Comparing prices is your insurance that you get the best deal possible. Getting advice is your insurance that you'll know as much as you can. Regular check-ups, dental exams, and financial reviews are your insurance that you'll discover a problem while it's still manageable. Insurance is your understanding that problems are part of life. And you protect yourself by insuring yourself against them.

Professionals, Experts, Counselors, and Know-It-Alls

From the President of the United States deciding on national policy to you asking a passerby for directions, everyone needs guidance. You need advice you can trust. You might be too close to the situation. Your emotions and unrelated details can distort the values. You lose direction, act irrationally, or avoid it. An advisor, personally unaffected by the situation, can give an objective opinion. They don't have the personal attachment or concern for the effort it takes. They see what works.

You may not know someone with the experience you need. Good intentions and common sense are available, a kind word or an extra hand. Friends help you the best they can. What if you have a legal question or health issue? Who do you ask then? You want someone with the right education and experience. You want a professional. You're willing to pay for their advice. It could be an accountant or a doctor. It could be a car mechanic or your personal trainer. They're consultants because the final decision is always yours. You just want to trust that their advice is in your best interests, at least from their point of view.

You want them to be right but you want them to be honest even when they're wrong. No one completely understands the nexus of issues that bring you to seek their help. Everyone's problems are a bit different, but all problems make sense. When you work with the right professional, you'll be talking to someone who deals with your kind of problem every day. You'll know they're good when they put your interests first.

You want your experts to love you. It sounds silly wanting your lawyer to love you but that's exactly what you need. You want them to care about you. When you look for an advisor, you want their knowledge *and* their concern for your well-being. If you don't feel it, move on. No matter how well recommended they are, you still have to trust them. There are many qualified counselors to choose from. Be wary of advisors who oversell themselves. Pompous self-importance is often a veil for poor performance.

You need good communication. You have to know how to use the advice you get. You want to trust that your advisor understands your problem including your attitude toward it. You really want a magical fix that's fast and cheap. But when you keep getting nowhere, creativity is your answer. You need new ideas and that may mean getting a new advisor.

That's crazy.

Happiness is a positive attitude focused on success even if it's just enjoying the weather. Disappointments pass then you reorient yourself to feeling good again. Your attitude is what matters. Your mind is independent. It can see the good in a bad situation and the problems in a good situation. It's usually real but not always. When you believe in an imagined problem it's still real to you. Your mind is a mish-mash of sensations, instincts, beliefs, thoughts, creations, evaluations, emotions, thoughts about your emotions, and the thoughts and feelings of everyone you're in contact with. However complex it gets, your mind is still guided by the perfection in your soul. Somewhere you know the truth.

Your soul is guided by love. Despite differences in personalities, the love in your soul binds you to everyone. But interpreting love can be divisive. You want peace with your neighbors but you may not like their home is painted some garish color. And they may not like your loud parties. Peace needs compromise. People need to make judgments about the material limits of love. Society wants a happy medium that supports its differences in an environment respectful of its culture. Personality types repeat in every culture; timid or aggressive, selfish or caring. You might question a cultural attitude but you'll understand its personalities.

You're a human being; a conscious, living soul. You're connected to God and the Universe through love, including all consciousness and materiality. You have an identity with humanity yet you're an independent soul with your own free will. You're a personality with interests and talents. Then nature pulls you this way and that and you mold yourself within it. You have your fate, the master plan for your soul in agreement with God's purpose for your life. Parts of your

100

plan are reasonable from a human point of view. Others are so extreme they only make sense from a spiritual point of view working your way through Creation. Some parts are God simply wanting to know more. And some parts, God only knows.

Everything works through your mind. Every thought, feeling, impression, sensation, inspiration, inclination, and lesson learned, assemble in your mind. You consider them alone and in combinations. Your trust is what your mind tells you to believe. Your values are the variations you believe are in your best interests. You always act in your best interests so it's important to have a healthy mind to rely on.

A healthy mind is honest. It knows the truth is dependable. A healthy mind is positive. It senses the faults in lies and misconceptions. A healthy mind is non-judgmental. It accepts human foibles. A healthy mind respects its environment and accepts reality. A healthy mind is self-reliant but values good advice. A healthy mind respects God's guidance and trusts your free will. Above all, a healthy mind is grateful for the love that supports you.

An unhealthy mind is fearful, angry, sad, and desperate. It's wild. It rejects life's process and need for control. You may need help finding your stability. Don't resist that need. The last piece of your emotional clarity may be in your decision to get help. You want to be sure you can identify a situation and turn it into what you want. You want to feel God's love. When things are confused, knowing you can still win is the sign of a healthy mind.

Gotta minute?

You control time through schedules. Time's limitlessness is turned into logical segments that make it measurable, like the days on a calendar. Then you create the limits that coordinate your purpose with nature's schedule, like the farmer who times their planting for the season with the best growing conditions. Socially, time coordinates cooperation; agreements when to meet to accomplish a common goal. Being at your job, a trip to the dentist, taking a bus, or dinner with friends are all agreements to be at a certain place at a certain time. You control time when you understand managing your schedule means balancing your priorities. It takes courage because sometimes you have to be in two places at the same time.

Nature's response to time is in its cycles. Fall becomes winter. Day becomes night. Everything grows until it dies and then is born again. Every living thing has its mating season with natural conditions that favor it. You have cycles too. The cycles you choose are in your values. You control time by fitting your values into nature's design. That's why so many people go to Florida in the winter.

You organize your time to match the ebb and flow of events. You schedule it. As your plan develops, time marks your progress. When things go well, time compresses and you move ahead of schedule. It affects everything so it's not always an advantage. Other parts of your plan may have to catch up, like when you're building a house and the lumber comes early and has to sit in the rain because the expected foundation hasn't been poured yet. Sometimes things are delayed and extend time. Delays are considered a problem but they don't have to be. Sometimes other parts of your plan can use the extra time like when a rained out ball game gives an injured player another week to heal. Your plan is an interaction of synchronized events. You control its unpredictability by giving it time.

Give things the time they need. How often have you rushed and caused a mistake that being patient would have caught? How many times have you left your cell phone on the kitchen table as you rushed out? The basic thing you forget is that you shouldn't rush. Your plan answers to time not convenience. Respect time and take as much as you need. You may need a better idea but you'll always have enough time.

Respecting others takes time to see what's fair. You listen to their concerns and they listen to yours. The time you spend on others is rightfully yours. You can spend it any way you wish. You can get whatever you want for it. You can serve two years in the Peace Corps or spend all night at a local bar. Mutual respect is measured in time because everyone uses it. Time is a tool. You don't want to be late for an appointment or waste your time waiting for someone who's arranged to meet you. You just want to know what's worthwhile when it takes your time.

Like food, you digest your time. Your engagements nourish you at different rates. Office gossip is fun but deserves less time than doing your work and keeping your job. With time, like eating, if you don't eat enough (or take enough time) you feel uncomfortable. If you eat too much, or take too much time, you feel uncomfortable. If you eat the wrong thing, or waste your time, you feel uncomfortable. You control your time by managing it the same way you respect your diet. You keep your body healthy by eating the right foods. You keep your attitude healthy by knowing the time you invest in anything is well spent.

You decide how much time is worth to you. The problem is when more than one thing needs your attention at the same time. You manage your time by setting priorities. Coordinating your time with others' priorities is the challenge. Love and common sense can usually make a good schedule. Regrets are common because there may not be enough time to do everything. You may have to make more time. So you get a five-year loan instead of three years to reduce the financial strain of your monthly payments. You use social media and email to stay in touch with friends instead of talking on the phone which can be inconvenient when you're busy. You free yourself by creating time.

It's up to you.

You're responsible for keeping your life on track. You know what you want. You know what it's worth to you. You know your priorities. You know your situation. You control what you can. What you can't, you adjust to as best you can. Congratulate yourself on meeting the world. Respect your decisions. You're the center of it all. Whatever's happening, whatever anyone tells you, whatever society accepts is secondary. Your opinion of yourself is what matters. That's where your happiness is. It's your dignity and comfort. It's the place where your life makes sense.

If you're concerned that you won't get it right, know that your responsibility to yourself is unavoidable. If not physically, at least in your attitude. Whatever leadership skills you're born with, God bless you. What you lack, you have to learn. Maturity takes you part of the way. Desire takes you the rest. It's the beauty in parenthood that teaches you leadership. Overnight, you become head of a household, responsible for the lives of others. What a miracle that the parent and child mature together with the adult always ahead in experience so they can teach the child. Being a leader means trusting what you know and having the courage to act appropriately. Successful results usually define leadership, but common sense and sincerity are its real measure.

Being a good leader doesn't mean everything goes your way. Life's a challenge or it wouldn't be worth your effort. God wants you to succeed. Though you interpret success differently, you share the same love. Without love, your accomplishments are hollow. And with love, the world is less important.

Your responsibility is to accept being the leader. It's never about someone else's responsibilities even when your success depends on them, like being the team coach. Sometimes things work out. Other times you do everything right but fail. Beyond doing what you think is right, there's nothing left but to trust your sincerity. Life teaches you how to manage your thoughts and feelings. You learn to trust yourself. You come to realize that you'll always have new opportunities and God's love will always support you.

Chapter 6
In Good Spirits

Spirituality: My Ace in the Hole

I've fallen down quite a bit but I was never allowed to fail. God was always there to see things didn't get too far out of hand. I fell into bad times but I was always pulled out. I see it as my training. I'm blessed with a close connection to God, not unique but closer than most people. I can sense my spirituality. I see how the material and spiritual worlds work together. I don't get lost in ceremony and interpretations. I'm straightforward about it.

I've been aware of my otherworldliness since I was eight years old. I've had many experiences to prove it to me. I've studied it and grew to understand the simplicity in my spirituality. Lesson after lesson taught by Spirit. I feel its presence and converse with it. Remember, I've experienced hallucinations and this is different. This is always positive. You have the same opportunity in your own prayers. Life is a spiritual experience guided by love. Love inspires everything. Human questions have a time limit. Spirit has the grace of eternity to answer its questions.

With all these good things, my past reminds me that everyone has their stuff. It could be an illness, a confused attitude, or a loved one's troubles beyond your ability to help them. I've learned that your soul gives your life value. One day you'll leave here and everything stays behind except the love you created. My testimony is; God is real. I want you to believe me so you'll explore it for yourself. There are many things you believe just because somebody told you. So why not believe me too?

You gotta love 'em.

Love happens. You attract it. Subconsciously, you choose it. It doesn't hit you like lightning on a cloudless day. You feel it with a kindred spirit. That connection feels good. That support is comforting. Love grows when you share it so love as much as you can. But respect who you love. You learn that your parents' love is different than a stranger's love. It's the same love but with a different commitment. As free as love is, you have to be wise how you use it.

God is love. You can feel it. In a way, you control it. You control the creative will God gave you. You decide how you'll express your love. God created you to explore Creation. *God wants to know what you discover!* When you touch love in your desires, you include God in your adventure. It's a partnership between two self-aware, creative forces. God is responsible to you. God appreciates this responsibility and loves you wholeheartedly. God's grace is everywhere. Expect God's support. You relate to God in everything you do. You connect to the Almighty by wanting to. That puts God's power in your hands, not through you alone but through your partnership.

Interpreting love is confusing because you're mixing your feelings with everyone else's. Still, it's amazing how successful it is. You might think another culture's concept of love is barbaric, yet every culture respects it. Every culture loves its maturing youth and has ceremonies for coming of age whether it's a walkabout through the Australian bush or a sweet sixteen party in Peoria. Love excites passion when you want it and elation when you have it. It's tangible. You can feel it in your body. You can't avoid its essence, the spiritual connection between you, God, and Creation. This is your challenge; to express love in agreement with your life.

Love is the connection. It's beyond description so we call it God. It's conscious, creative, and free. It makes you sensible and wise. You can feel its power and comfort. Everything is love. You're a seed in its consciousness. Love takes care of itself, including you. It wants to be your friend. Love is the power of positive interaction. It interprets differences and finds the common ground. It gives and receives. It guides you. It makes you complete. It responds to you. It's as delicate as a butterfly and as bright as the Sun. It's as life affirming as a kind word or missing it, can make you miserable with self-doubt. It's everything you are and all you hope to be. It's the measure of everything. It's the value in anything. It's the responsibility in your soul.

God, who art in heaven?

"Do you believe in God?" That's how the conversation starts. Then it moves to your religious upbringing and the paradox of why God allows so much pain in the world. What exactly is an omnipotent God? What does God want? What's its value to you? Why do some people cling to their beliefs like it was the only thing keeping them from damnation and others see it as a simple complement to their lives? People are different. Attitudes are different. One's not right and the other one wrong. Life's an examination of consciousness. Every perspective has its value. There are personality types, cultural types, and vocational types. There's you and seven billion like you sharing this experience. Free will allows an exotic mix. Creation's consciousness imbues each atomic particle with love. These particles combine to create opportunities. As you touch your spirituality, you can sense the unity in things. God's interest is to understand itself in the same way you try to understand yourself. That's why you ask so many questions.

Where did you come from? Some people make the argument for evolution. Others make the argument for creationism. Some people think human beings come from an extra-terrestrial intervention. *Why can't they all be true?* There's no rule that one excludes the others. Divine intervention can evolve. The argument for extra-terrestrials is there are no other creatures here like human beings so that could make sense. The Universe is a big place. Conscious life on this planet is enough to believe there's conscious life elsewhere. Just remember; love is the same everywhere.

You exist. You love. You choose. You're a surrogate for God's creativity in exploring itself. You're important. You're perfect, but not like some current fashion. You're perfect as a creative force. You can make life anything you want. God's plan explores the priorities you choose for your survival. What would you sacrifice to accomplish your goal? Would you invest ten years in an education to have an interesting career? Or would you give up everything and live begging handouts to simplify your life? Someone may go on a hunger strike to draw attention to their cause, but how often do you see a homeless person refusing food? So which is the greater sacrifice: to accept death for a cause or to accept death because you give up? Wanting the best for yourself is the essence of free will. Your worst choice still comes from your desire to improve yourself. With all your freedoms, you still can't disappear. You can never dismiss your soul.

No matter how complicated things get, you're never alone. You're never without God's love and attention. You're a point of view, an inspiration in God's mind. Your connection to God is unbreakable. The same mind that formed the Universe formed you. Even the thought that things are connected is a misnomer. Creation is one entity. There is no separation. God is one. Nature makes things seem separate. Individualization creates opportunities for the exploration of Creation. You solve the puzzle when you see the parts as one picture. Love is the energy in everything.

And Now Introducing God, the Deity; the One and Only

The One, but which one? Human beings idealize God as a personality, someone they can relate to in human terms. God takes a form palatable to the culture. God's interpretation in an intimate tribal culture is different from how masses of humanity love each other in the competitive anonymity of today's modern cities. The social contract is different, but God is the same. Love is the same. That's why when you meet a stranger, you know what to expect. In love and survival everyone's understandable.

God is the Creator. Creation is confusing, but it has to make sense somehow or there'd be no need to question it. The constant is knowing God's love is everywhere. Your beliefs come from questioning God's values and learning how to react. You pray for answers. God helps you find them. The answers have to be practical because life is practical. You need loving answers you can use. What you learn about loving is how you measure your success.

Religion focuses on *how* to believe in God. Different concepts are explored to explain the relationship between you and your faith. Whichever prophet you esteem, they all have a moral code. No matter how accurate it is or what you call it, if it's sincere then it's a suitable path to your partnership with God. Religion is your conscious awareness of God. It's your consciousness of self-discovery, unity, and love. God's description doesn't change its nature. God's existence isn't a convenience to one point of view. God is what it is. Its proof is that there are so many people who believe in God.

Your desire to know God is like a knock on the door. "Are you there, God? Who are you, God? What do you want from me, God?" Your sincerity is enough to start. The purpose of religion is to inspire you to ask questions, to bring you back into union with God with no illusion of separation. Then you can ask about pain and purpose, personal responsibility, and the meaning of success. Get started. Live your life with inspiration. Love yourself. The Universe supports you even when you don't like where it takes you. Medicine doesn't always taste like candy, but it usually makes you feel better.

How you relate to God each moment is what really counts. It's not the dramatic "God, please don't let my child be sick!" moment. Everyone wants help when they're desperate. What's important is seeing your connection to God in your everyday thoughts. You have common sense to know what's right and forgiveness to end your problems and start again. You have God's love in you. You have the promise of happiness. You have time and commitment. You have God's wisdom and strength. All religions serve the same purpose. You decide which is best for you. It's not about rules and ceremonies. It's about the love that parallels all religions. When you find your faith, God will show you how to use it.

I will always love you.

Devotion is your commitment to God. It's how you value your responsibilities. It can be formal or casual. It can be your whole life or a thought now and then. Your belief gives it value, whether or not you accept it or even believe it's real. Your intent defines it. It's not a quid pro quo. It's not an investment where you expect a return from God on the effort you put in your prayers. It's not your alignment with some interpretation of God. Your desire to share God's love makes you whole. Love can support every thought you have. Faith personifies the trust in your devotion. You're investing in a sure thing. You're putting your trust in love.

Devotion isn't a trade. God doesn't need repayment. God appreciates your consideration, but it isn't required. God enjoys sharing love. Devotion is you loving God back. Rituals are satisfying. They pull you out of your routine to a spiritual place that helps you focus on God. In that moment, your survival disappears replaced by love. But it can't be an act. A sincere thought while you're brushing your teeth is more valuable than all the posing in the world. Religious practice is a bridge. It's a conduit between your physical and spiritual selves. The true altar of devotion is you.

Devotion is personal but it comes with social responsibilities. The question is, "Do you follow your heart or follow the group?" All ideals are wise. Common sense is wise. Love is wise. But some, who identify by their religion, resist love because it's hard to trust when it isn't validated by their beliefs. They find comfort in the dogma and traditions they trust. Religions are the result of divine influence given to human beings to explore. It's easy to understand why there can be problems finding common ground when people's needs are different. You have to cross a gulf of disbelief to accept a new belief. Ask yourself, "Can your survival be trusted to God in a way other than what you believe now?" That's why understanding love is important. It allows you to consider alternatives without disturbing your faith.

Devotional rituals are different. It's your belief that your respectful behavior connects you to God. Acts of sacrifice, whether it's volunteering at church or flailing yourself bloody in a religious parade are essentially the same. Your act asks God to recognize your respect. Your devotions may be in ecstatic dancing freeing you from worldly concerns or separating yourself from mainstream thinking by living in a religious commune. It's common to find devotion in prayer or reading something spiritually uplifting. Another common theme is service. Religions find helping others crystallizes their devotion, whether it's preaching on a street corner or feeding the homeless. Charity is the material expression of devotion. It recognizes the unity in everything and the practical consideration that you serve God when you serve others. They're all great but true devotion only asks that you consider God in what you do.

World Within a World: Your Body & Soul

What does your soul do? In a human being, your soul joins with your body to explore life's aspect of Creation. Then what happens when you die? Do you disperse into nothingness or does your soul's memory survive? Do you still have responsibilities? Obviously, you're done with your body. What about your thoughts and feelings? Thoughts and feelings relate to your actions, like the time you were fired or the log home you dreamed of building in Vermont. They relate to the physical world. They express mental energy, the atomic structure of your thoughts waiting to be physically formed. This is your brain function, the reality of your thoughts, feelings, and instincts. Life is its reality. But consciousness is your eternal soul's awareness. Its reality is love. You join your body and soul together through love.

Consider existence as a single thought. You're part of it. You connect to everything as an individual able to express your will in the exploration of consciousness. God became self-aware. It was new and unknown. So you're designed to explore the unknown. That's why you love questions, game shows, sporting events, and mysteries. Answering the unknown is inherent to your nature. That's why you're desperate to know "Who won?" when it really doesn't mean anything. The beauty is you communicate with it all. Nothing is separate from you. The connection between you and everything else is your sixth sense.

That begs the question, "Why?" You want to "succeed" but nature is about survival. People give up when they feel they're a failure at survival, not because life doesn't interest them. Life's a challenge. That's its purpose. Like going through paint samples to pick what color to paint your bedroom, it presents layers of options to choose from. It's not meant to beat you. Love makes you who you are, whole with everything there is. Individuality fools you into thinking you're alone, but it's not real. God's consciousness always includes you.

Wealth makes survival easy. It gives you the freedom to create what you want and explore your life without the burden of wondering how you're going to pay your bills. Competition with nature, including other human beings, makes it confusing. How do you express your purpose in concert with your responsibility to love the world? What's fair? You come to realize love is innately successful. Love is your stability. Real wealth is your success at keeping your soul balanced between love and what you think you need to survive.

Holy Mackerel

Holiness is God's presence in everything. It's common to revere God's holiness in a religious icon or some event you see as a miracle. The truth is if you believe in God then you're consciously connected to God's holiness. You may admire a religious figure who's devoted their whole life to understanding humanity's relationship to God. You may think they're closer to God than you'll ever be. Anyone who invests that much time should certainly know God better. But you have the same opportunity. You can know God. Your desire to feel God's presence is your own holy experience.

Holy objects *can help* you on your path to God. In holy places or the presence of holy objects, you can *feel* you're in the presence of God. Your reciprocal energy closes the circle as you release your love in the same way you feel awe in the quiet of a grand cathedral. You trust the physical world so you want physical ways to explain God's love. It's hard to believe what a stranger tells you and blindly follow them as the right way to live. The trappings of gold tassels and clerical robes make appealing theater but do they prove anything? You need proof that satisfies your common sense. Whether it's a holy book or religious charm, holy objects serve that purpose. They command reverence if for no other reason than they align with what you believe. They serve as spiritual focal points to share with others. Holy objects represent ideals, the epitome of everything positive that makes you who you are.

The spirit world is supernatural. It just means its nature is different from what you're used to. Like any mystery, you hope for a glimpse of it. Conscious contact with spirit is so rare that any opportunity to experience it is revered. Precious are the prophets who brought God's guidance in an intelligible form that established the foundation for the world's religions. People honor their bones and clothing, anything close to them, anything they touched. It's easier to trust something physical. Spirit is a different state of mind. It sends you messages only your soul understands. Then it enters your life as the wisdom that makes it practical. A thing is holy because you honor its connection to love. Love makes everything holy.

A sacrilege rejects love. When you can't accept love, your confusion becomes disdain for what others feel is sacred. In truth, love makes you a human being. Love has answers you can't find anywhere else. Life is a mystery, an insecurity. That motivates you to understand it. Just assume that what your soul needs is here. With effort you *can* understand it. To deny your confusion doesn't resolve it. Dismissing reality doesn't end your responsibility. Sacrilege is a convenient tool for rationalizing your temporary superiority over your soul. For the short time of your life, you can avoid the work it takes to know what you're feeling.

Really, you decide what's holy. Do you have faith enough to trust yourself with such a responsibility? Can you see God's love? Will it be at your bedroom altar, in your heart as you look out over the ocean, or in a keepsake from someone you love? Maybe holiness is nothing more than your desire to live a loving life. That, without doubt, is holy.

Heaven & Hell, Now and Again

Heaven and Hell are simple references to help you evaluate your life. Have you made the right choices and you're going to Heaven or did you have a bad attitude and you're going to Hell? Holiness comes from the love you create, the love you give and the love you receive. Your millions of individual choices aren't that important. Every decision you make is a value judgment. You weigh the pros and cons then choose what you think works best. You know you can't have everything or make everyone happy. There are advantages and disadvantages to every decision. Even your best choice can have a disappointing consequence. But what else can you do? Life's a paradox. Heaven's image of pleasant comforts versus Hell's fiery misery is meant to help make your choices easier. But who's to say, *whatever the result*, you weighed your choices well?

You want comfort. Your soul wants peace. Your soul looks past your life. There's comfort in traditions that help explain what to expect when you die. Every religion has beliefs on eternity. Those beliefs help you question how to live your life. But only love can grant you peace. Look at Hell. With eternal damnation as the benchmark, could love make that misery go away? Yes. What other purpose could pain serve? Love replaces misery. Through your free will, you choose love or misery. Does that mean your soul might suffer forever? What logical purpose would that serve? God is practical. Your soul must be able to have regrets and then be able to choose a better path. Misery isn't about punishment. It's about opportunities to create love.

Heaven and Hell explain how your behavior determines your future. Success in life is apparent, but who can say what eternity values? Beyond doing your best, you have to trust fate to give you a good result. Life's a moral mish-mash with conflicting religious views, changing social norms, cultural traditions, politics, and assorted emotional stresses, all interpreted by your creative, free will. Right and wrong bend with the wind. There's one motivation that's right in any situation. Love guides right behavior. Your desire to find a fair balance is what makes you successful even when you're disappointed with the result. Humanity is about survival, but even enemies know love. With love, everyone's on common ground.

Then how do you get to Heaven? How do you find peace for your soul? How can you be satisfied with your life? Righteousness aligns with love so if you're a loving person then Heaven must be where you are. And if reincarnation is real, do Heaven and Hell even exist? Is eternity an end or the base for a new experience? Is it possible that you live multiple lives under changing conditions? Like any educational experience, change inspires your creativity. With each lifetime your soul samples a new situation. From being a cannibal to jumping into a volcano to appease the gods, you're bound to learn something. Multiple lives give you fresh ways to understand love. That's the continuing mystery, "How does love create your life?"

Evil: A Layman's Look at the Devil

Evil takes pleasure in other people's suffering. It's an aberration, a confusion about humanity's purpose. It misses the connection love makes between you and Creation. It ignores the love in others. It's selfishness beyond reason. Evil materializes selfishness and sees people as objects. It sees others as disposable. It values its own gratification at any cost...to someone else. It sees love's pleasures without recognizing the consciousness of love that makes every soul beautiful. Evil separates itself from love for being impractical and sees no value in fairness and support.

The term "evil" is a warning label, like a skull and crossbones on a box of poison. It's more of an opinion because it's hard to judge others and the choices they've had to make. But no one wants to associate with evil. It contradicts God. The question is, "Is a behavior evil or just contrary to accepted values?" Is describing something as evil the truth or an extreme statement made to create an aversion in its audience? Many conflicts have sincere people on both sides. Following their beliefs, people regularly do awful things to each other as every war attests. But is it evil or a sacrifice of normal values to a greater cause? It can be the most troubling question you ask yourself as your only redemption is in accepting responsibility no matter what your reason.

"Sin" is a word used to caution people not to act against God's will. The problem is it's someone's presumption to interpret God's will. From a religious standpoint, it's worthwhile as a convenience to institutionalize positive, social behavior. But when it's judgmental, it takes on importance greater than its purpose and can paralyze your creativity into dogmatic traditions. Sin is any material substitute for love, whether it's food, sex, possessions, or adulation. It looks for meaning in the material world when you don't trust love. Love is the only judge of sin. God's grace is its justice.

Demons, Lucifer, Satan, and many other personifications of evil I believe are real. They represent a willful resistance to God. The details are conjecture. How it affects you is what matters. Don't worry. Their influence can't control you. At worst, it's a nuisance creating unneeded doubts. Nothing negative can bother you if you reject it. God's will is absolute. God's love for you is real. If a demon annoys you, like some bothersome bee, ignore it and it'll go away. Then how do you separate a demon's influence from your honest doubts? There's a subtlety to a demon's negativity that tries to influence your thinking. They show up when you're tired, stressed out, or feeling bad. That's their opening. Trust your faith. Trust love. If you have a positive attitude, no demon can ever find a place in your thoughts.

You have power over evil. You can usually find some measure of joy even if it's just enjoying a quiet lunch. You wake up each day looking for your purpose. Outside, every soul is doing their best to answer their purpose. Everyone wants to be successful. Love makes you successful. Love supports Creation's achievements and repels evil's destructiveness. Love makes sense of everything.

The Clergy's Touch

The clergy's job is to help you learn to trust love amid life's chaos. They act as a liaison between God, their beliefs, and you. Their role deserves respect. There's a charitable aspect that they give up their "material values" to serve others with no thought of payment for their time. They're not superior. They share your foibles. They share your needs. They've volunteered for a life of service. They work at their religion. They invest their time so they can help you choose your values. Love is their guide. If it wasn't, there'd be no need for religion.

Religion is needed. While the priestly class may have an aptitude for it, you can really do it yourself. You can live a life honoring God. Even if you don't believe in God, you still need a moral code of conduct that respects society's rules if you want to be part of it. The clergy's plan aligns your spiritual responsibilities with your social responsibilities. But you may not feel connected to it. It could be your personality is inclined to a different point of view. The clergy's job is to remind you that the other end of the connection is God.

Their job is to intercede with God on your behalf and help you direct your attention towards God. They stand behind you, grab you by the shoulders, and point you in the right direction. It's that simple. Regardless of their beliefs, creating a conscious relationship between you and God is their purpose. Do they make mistakes? You wouldn't be human if you didn't make mistakes. The ideals of their purpose are still correct. Trying to simplify life's paradoxes into beliefs you can trust is a good thing.

The clergy is charitable. They care for your welfare. They want to help you. They want to inspire you. Survival takes work. Your spirit likes it that way. You like a challenge, whether it's learning to drive or raising your kids. If your life doesn't challenge you, you'll find a goal that does. Your purpose is to make sense of life's trials. Think about your job and family. They make you ask questions. The clergy reminds you that God helps you answer those questions.

Cults & The New Age

Your quest for enlightenment isn't a cult because some doubter says, "That's too odd. It must be a cult." A cult is a spiritual movement whose organization becomes greater than its philosophy. Its leadership becomes more important than its adherent's desire to love themselves. In a cult, you believe wisdom is outside yourself instead of a personal responsibility. Guidance is a direction, not an achievement. Your achievement comes from your decisions about what you learn. A cult ignores the love that attracted its members and replaces it with disciplines. Every religion begins under God's direction to explain love as it resonates with a part of humanity. The cultural environment dictates its needs. Your spiritual experience must be explained in light of those needs. Societies evolve. Religions grow with them. Any religion can serve a new perspective if it answers life's questions through love. Then the new design works.

The New Age is a mélange of intriguing spiritual and psychological phenomena. It's an examination of what it means to be human. It includes western religions, eastern sects, shamanism, ancient beliefs, astrology, extra-terrestrials, channeling, divination, psychic awareness, psychological techniques, physical regimens, meditation, prayer, the afterlife, and more than I know. Most have been around awhile with new perspectives arising as personal explorations hit pay dirt. People have always shared their thoughts about life. Some are so strange it's a wonder where they find them. For the New Age, nothing's off limits if it's an honest understanding of Creation. Usefulness is judged by performance. Like a new hair restorer, are you getting the benefit promised? Anything that helps, you'll accept.

You want control. New Age thinking is a good way to have it. You choose the parts that appeal to you. You may resonate better with a physical regimen like yoga over the emotional calming aspect in chanting. Or you might find your peace looking for the mathematical logic in Creation. Religions separate into physical, emotional, and psychological practices. It's how you relate to life no matter what your belief. Every religion is a system. From that base, you mold your personality into something that satisfies your soul. Your soul's growth is your purpose. Unconditional love is the path to peace. Your challenge is to see love everywhere.

Society is more materially well off than ever. Convenience abounds. It gives you more freedom to think creatively. Thinking has evolved. There's freedom in New Age thinking that isn't available in traditional religions. I was part of the New Age. I met many good people doing the same thing. That was the fun of it. You got together with ten people and three were channels and the other seven psychics. I grew with it. I formed a point of view. Everyone should have a point of view. Education isn't endless. You graduate when you find your confidence. The purpose of the New Age is to engage God and understand love. That's what life's about. Could I have done it more conventionally? That's the beauty of it. Everything's included. The New Age isn't a philosophy. It's your intention to support your consciousness no matter where it takes you.

118

God's Magic: Miracles

Miracles prove God's awareness. They demonstrate God's support. A miracle hands you the answer on a silver platter. But why do you have problems that need a miracle to fix? Problems test you, but not beyond your limits. There's no benefit in that. God loves you. Miracles give you solutions that may defy logic but make perfect sense to God. Life's an exercise, not a judgment. When things go beyond your ability, God intercedes to help you. A miracle isn't a way to avoid responsibility. You can't paint God into a corner, give up, and think, "Now you fix it God!" You don't command miracles, but you can't avoid them. God won't let you suffer. God's support often comes in a way that hands responsibility back to you. One way or another you're going to deal with your problems. Re-tailoring your trials is just another miracle.

Miracles show God's love in a dramatic way. They may glimmer in subtlety or shine so bright you have to close your eyes but they all reveal God's work in your life. You could say your life is a series of miracles. Every breath you take is a miracle that keeps you alive. You're so close to miracles that it's easy to miss them. When you reserve the word "miracle" for something seemingly impossible that conveniently happens to help you, you miss the point. It may be as simple as a quick turn that helps you avoid an accident. The problem with the miracle of a narrow escape is again, "Why was there a need for an escape in the first place?" Why do you need a dangerous encounter for God to show up and save you? Because it gets your attention. God doesn't want your gratitude. God wants your questions. God doesn't want you to be awed. God wants you to ask, *"Why?"*

You like miracles. They're better than problems. You can miss crashing into a tree by half an inch and it's a miracle you didn't die. But why did so many things come together to put you in danger? Why did you have to be in that place at that time? Why were you distracted? Why was the weather like it was? You live with things you can't control. You count on yourself to do your best. You make things happen, or so you think. You still have limits no matter how skillful you are. Your fate, the spiritual theme for your life, is a multiple-choice test with unlimited answers. You take the test every day and fill in the boxes in the time you have. When you lose your way, God sends you "miracles." Miracles aren't to give you relief. Miracles are to help you see your opportunities.

Miracles highlight, "Look how close you came to failure but everything's alright now." A miracle isn't an antidote. A miracle is a lesson for you to accept a new attitude. Life easily absorbs your consciousness so a miracle must be emphatic to get your attention. They lay the groundwork through some frightful hardship then raise God's glory to save you. So take a breath, enjoy the gift, then figure out how to use it.

You received a gift. Whatever you feared is whole again. You experienced a miracle. Through God's grace your hopes were fulfilled. Dramatic happenings are the treasure of God's wisdom specifically meant for you. A miracle isn't a moment in time. It's part of a process. You can be thankful for it and go on your way. Or you can ask more of your miracles. You can take them apart and glean the lessons they have for you. A miracle isn't a free pass. It's a wake-up call.

Faith: Trust in God is trust in life.

Faith is your trust in love. It's the theme for your relationship with God. It's your spiritual investment. Your spiritual consciousness has absolute faith. It's naturally who you are. You don't have to work at it. But life needs proof you can trust. You want love to make physical sense. You want to be confident that your beliefs perform the same way every time. You depend on them. To put your trust in something untouchable requires faith, something you question but still accept.

Faith is love's unity. It's the connection between you and everything else. It connects you to animals, vegetables, and far off galaxies. It connects you to your family, work, and interests. It connects you to your country, religion, and culture. It connects you to human beings everywhere. Without even knowing them, you easily understand their lives. Totally and individually, faith connects you to God.

Faith says to trust love. Does that mean you should trust everyone because you share God's love? Yes and no. You know God's love is there, but you still have to protect yourself from human nature. Human nature shows you people can be selfish and resentful. They lie, cheat, steal, make mistakes, and avoid responsibilities. Still, God won't fail you. Love is greater than all those things. Human foibles are the shadow of life's challenges. Temporal humanity can never defeat your soul. Your humanity serves your spirituality. In this environment, your success is measured by the love you create; the love you give and the love you receive.

Think about your failures and successes. Think how hard it is to control your life and keep a positive attitude. Succeed or fail, you'll doubt whatever you do until you know for sure. That's the game. You're a human being confronted by survival, not the eternal love you're used to. The miracle is how God helps you. Your life is God's design. Your soul isn't measured by fame, good looks, or your bank account. It's measured by the love in your life. With common sense, you can release the material concepts you cling to and learn to trust the life God gave you. Your spirit's experience is worth the price. Your faith says you agree.

Yes. You can have it.

Hope is the belief that love will get you what you want. Hope aligns your desires with love's support. It's your belief that you're entitled to what you want even when what you get is different from what you expect. Your soul's purpose is on God's schedule. Delays can make you doubt your hopes. Real hope trusts patience. Hope respects common sense but trusts love over the idea that perfection is the answer to everything. You can do everything right and still fail. You can trip and stumble but still succeed. Hope respects your sincerity, not your resources. It inspires you to move forward regardless of events. Hope achieves your spiritual purpose, not a trivial distraction like a ball game score or a compliment from a stranger. Hope aligns your desires with God's plan.

Hope is a win-win situation. When you believe in God's plan, what could be better than God blessing your success? Free will defines your nature. You can choose whatever you want for any reason you like. The gift of a clever mind will guide you down one path while a debilitating illness will force you down a much harder road. However your life takes shape, success is about your judgments and values. But whatever you choose, God will always ask the same question, "How is love a part of your decision?"

When you respect love in your desires you include God in your plans. It means you shouldn't be afraid. God is near. God's love is as real as opening your eyes in the morning. There's no other requirement. You're already whole with God. So see God's love in everything. God communicates to you as your day's lesson might be to slow down if you keep bumping into things. It doesn't deny you. It helps you set a better pace. God speaks to you every day, but you still have to listen.

Is hope enough to give you what you want? Yes, in the sense that everything starts with hope. Then will your dreams fall into your lap? Yes, but it won't seem like it. It'll seem like hard work, disappointment, unrewarded perseverance, and the need for constant self-encouragement. Your idea of success may be different from the success your soul sees. Of course, if you work hard, you'll probably get what you want one way or another. But do you really need millions of dollars or would having that money just make you feel like you've accomplished something respectable? Is finding the perfect mate what you think it is or are you too immature to weather the storms of human nature that forge a marriage? Some people seem to have everything. Others seem to have nothing. Love makes everyone equal. Hope is love's ability to make God your willing partner. God will give you what you really want.

Making Love Real

Charity's purpose is to share love. Charity expresses the value in love. When someone's having a hard time, you try to make their life easier. You help push their car out of the snow or give sincere advice. You're glad to help however you can. Your love is embodied in those gifts. Sympathy and spiritual encouragement are great but you have material needs. You have to feel secure in your survival before you can introspectively address your soul's purpose. Charity shares support. Life is your soul's adventure, so you must succeed at survival. It can be overwhelming even when you make the right decisions. Charity brings love to life. Charity is love's physical element, blessed in giving and receiving.

Helping others feels good. Your generosity helps remove the limits that confine them to their circumstances. It's a stretch to make generosity a priority for your resources. You have your own problems and life is expensive. But there are practical reasons to help your community when people ask you to contribute. Youth and seniors programs, helping those with disabilities, and beautification projects help you too. But what about helping strangers who've experienced the miseries of war, famine, plagues, natural disasters, or economic downturns, things that send whole societies into ruin. Your charitable gifts reach from your heart to the heart of a stranger to alleviate the desperation that binds them to their hardships and in your kindness connects you to God.

Charity is a two-way street. You give with grace and receive with gratitude. It's an opportunity to create love. You don't like a situation that puts you on the receiving end of charity but respect it. Your pride in self-reliance is honorable, but everyone needs help time to time whether it's a bankrupt city or a single mother living in the streets. Charity means you need help beyond your means. Resistance to charity makes no sense. If you had to lift something too heavy for you, would you think asking for help is charity? It's just someone giving you a hand to achieve something you need. Today you benefit. Tomorrow they benefit. When you refuse charity, you take away another person's chance to share their love. Charity is inclusive. It's love as a social institution. Charity's purpose isn't life-long maintenance. You're not on Easy Street if you need help. Charity's goal is to help you move past your problems. The motive for giving or receiving charity is your respect for yourself when you realize the bond between human beings is love.

Your Life as a Prayer

Prayer sets the tone for your relationship with God. Your prayers invite God to join you as a partner. Your prayers welcome God's guidance. Prayer is real communication. Through prayer you give life to your relationship with God. Prayer isn't begging, though sometimes it's desperation that leads you to pray. Prayer is a cooperative effort where like minds work to achieve a common goal, your success as a human being. Are you equal to God? As far as free will goes, you are. You're designed to be. It's your purpose. God loves free will. It allows you to question things from your own perspective. It's how you create your life. That's why including God in your life matters. It values God's involvement and says, "You're welcome here." God likes the invitation. God likes working with you.

You might formalize your prayers through some religious practice. Religious ceremonies take you away from your routines to help you focus on God. But it's hard to be sincere when a ceremony is your only prayer. I pray all day long. I live my life as a prayer. My thoughts always include God. I share my wishes and my gratitude. I don't pray for things unless someone's having a bad time who I think needs God's attention. It's like when someone says, "I'll pray for you." It's a powerful gift. I pray to improve my character. I feel those qualities will get me what I want. I'm grateful for the help and I accept the work. That's my side of the bargain. If I feel insincerity in myself, any mechanical response, I keep repeating it till I know it's from my heart. I ask God to keep an eye on me. I complain when God sends me problems I feel are too much for me. And I always call God *"Boss."*

It's not how much you pray that matters. It's the sincerity in your prayers that reaches God's ear. I saw a TV evangelist proudly proclaim he had people praying twenty-four hours a day. I thought, "Is twenty-four hours better than twenty-three hours?" I reduced it till I thought, "Is two seconds of prayer better than one second?" The answer is the time you pray doesn't matter. It's a human concept that more is better. With prayer, it's quality over quantity. It's your sincerity, as much as a grain of mustard seed, that God values. God respects your sincerity. God values your faith in your prayers.

I had a vision. I was in a room facing a wall. It was pitch-black, no light at all, but every time I said a prayer, a small hole punched in the wall and a ray of light streamed in. I kept praying and more and more holes appeared with more and more light coming in. I realized there was a better way than doing it a prayer at a time. I could take down the wall. I did and God's love filled the room. The darkness disappeared. Try it. Instead of making your connection to God in solitary prayers, take down the wall between you and God and live your life as a prayer. When you include God in your decisions, your life becomes a prayer.

Do something!

Service exemplifies charity. It values your efforts to help someone in need. But you don't give love the same way you give a coat. The money you give helps, but the thought behind your donation matters. It's your love. It's like a telethon where a big corporation gives a million dollars to a charity but the company sees it as a marketing tool. It's okay that they see it as advertising. They want their customers to know they're good citizens and a benefit to the community. They want you to do business with them. There's nothing wrong with that. Then a child comes up and gives all the money they made selling newspapers, a few hundred dollars, and the announcer says, "It's the thought that counts." Well, they're right. It's the love that counts.

You feel good when you give money to help those in need. Sharing connects you to your responsibilities as a human being. When you participate in a charity, you give of yourself. Money is just part of it. Human beings are consumers and people with problems need their problems addressed along with their daily needs. Charities don't generate enough cash to pay for everything. They need donations. They need money to fulfill their mission. The beauty is service leaps over the financial issue and goes directly to solving the problem. It works through people like you doing things the charity needs without paying for your services. The stories about monks making wine and paying their way are charming but rare in today's society.

Sharing love through service is limitless because kindness and need are limitless. Service organizes it. Service is synergistic. It creates more than the love you put into it. It increases with every person it touches. The task doesn't matter. Making a phone call or sitting with someone who needs a kind word are the simple tasks of service. Service isn't a burden. It's an opportunity. Service may mean asking others for money instead of just giving your own. Maybe you sell a raffle ticket. Someone has to do it. Expenses reduce the benefits a charity can give so your service increases what the charity can do. Not everyone can be a Good Samaritan. You share what you can. If you have the time and energy, it's satisfying to give of yourself. You're around good people and you know you're doing something for someone who needs your help.

Thanks a lot!

You say "Thank you." when you're grateful. You want that person to know they matter to you. What they did made your life easier. Their sacrifice, no matter how small, helped you. You reinforce your connection. You increase your harmony together. You want them to know they can count on you too. You show your gratitude through respect; a kind word or gift. It's your heartfelt consideration. People sense it. Gratitude is friendship. It manifests the love between you.

How do you show gratitude for God's attention? How do you reciprocate God's love? What can you do for God? Wanting to do something is the start. Knowing it's possible is next. Gratitude connects you to God. God gives you love. When you receive God's love, you complete the cycle of gratitude. It unifies the love in your faith. Love is the only thing that satisfies God. Sure, you can light a candle to show your devotion or do community service. Those show gratitude in your intention to love God. Real gratitude comes from your soul. It's not repayment for anything. It's a friend respecting a friend. God doesn't need things. God only needs your love.

Gratitude comes from loving life. But what if your life's too hard? Managing your attitude is essential to your gratitude. You have the challenge of your own survival. You have the challenge of your purpose. It may not be desirable but life is always manageable. But why thank God for your miseries? You thank God for the opportunity to meet your problems in an environment where you can't fail...eternity. You work with love within life's turmoil. Life's tragedies are real and the suffering can be unbearable. Your blessing is the continuity of God's love. When you die, your soul doesn't disappear. You go on through eternity. Come to terms with life's hardships and be grateful. Sometimes you have to risk your faith and choose love over something more tangible. Fortunately, love makes your gratitude real.

You thank God for letting you play the game. It's proof that you trust the game. In the end, it's not about success or failure. Only one team wins the championship, later to be forgotten when the season starts again. Success *is how* you play the game. Values matter. Love is the measure. Love is in your gratitude.

Grace: It's hard being human.

Grace respects the difficulty in your choices. Sometimes you have to choose what you're willing to lose. The money you make working may be more important to you than taking a vacation. Grace respects your priorities and helps you understand your conflicts. Grace respects that you make honest mistakes. Through Grace, God understands your desire to be responsible isn't always enough. Grace is more than God's forgiveness. Grace is God's gratitude for your service to Creation.

You honor God's Grace by accepting it. When things are more than you can handle, God's Grace is with you. Through Grace, God fulfills its responsibility to your partnership. There's peace in God's Grace. There's gentleness in its power. In Grace, love is refined into forgiveness, its elemental meaning, the absence of blame, and human concerns disappear leaving the sweetness of love to restore your faith. The closest a human being can come to the essence of God is through Grace.

The message in Grace is that no matter how chaotic your life is, God supports you. You're never alone hanging off a cliff. Your problems serve God's purpose. When you get off track, God's there to help you. Grace is God saying, "Okay. That's enough now. Let's try something new." God's Grace is your relief.

God's Grace connects you physically to love's perfection. God intercedes in your life to create conditions that help you. You can jump from failure to success in an instant with the good news about your medical tests. Through Grace, you join with God to create a bond of appreciation. God makes it clear that whatever the problem, God is there for you. Grace connects you to God in an emotional peace more satisfying than victory. Through Grace God reminds you, "You're doing fine. Nothing can stop you."

Dogma, Opinion, & Belief

Why are there so many religions? How can the same thing be explained in so many ways? Whose idea of God is right? The essence of religion is to define love and the meaning of right behavior. If you think love can lead you to right behavior, I agree. Whether right behavior can lead you to love; I think it can. But the behavior itself doesn't matter. It's your intention to do the right thing that leads you to love.

A religion respects its culture. It aligns love with its social system. Most people believe they have a spiritual purpose. Then why wouldn't everyone think alike if love is the same everywhere? You live the same life. You make a living and enjoy what you love. But the imposition of a single way to love God challenges your creativity. It's confronting because you have to trust your life to it and everyone may not agree.

You respect your religion. You do your best to trust it. Often, when you feel strong, you trust yourself better to solve your problems. You enjoy religion's traditions more than you trust its prayers. It's something you belong to, like an extended family. But when you're out of control, your religious beliefs may be all you have. You can't control your life so in desperation you try to control God. That's not faith. That's not trust in love. Religion is a great tool but it's not an end in itself. Religion isn't instant gratification. Religion is to help you decide if your faith can make God real to you.

128

God makes sense in your soul's consciousness. The defining moment of your life is when you infuse your love with God's will. From the rainforests of the Amazon to the grand, stone churches of Manhattan, human beings pray to a higher power. Whatever you call it, through religion, you respect it. Every religion implores the Almighty, "God, help us do the right thing." When there's a space between your spiritual awareness and life's distractions, you need help, literal beliefs with miracles that prove they come from God. Those beliefs are your "religion."

The message of religion is that love serves all religions. You don't need the wisdom of a saint to see it. Human beings need help to understand their agreement with God. Different perspectives show that all religions meet in love. "What's God look like from where you are?" you might ask. Different personality types in different environments have different values and need different answers. Don't fear an unfamiliar religion. Each one has its purpose. The problem is the intolerance of those who place religious practice above love. Religion isn't a way to legitimize yourself. Religion is a definition that explains your life through love.

Do you see me, God? Can you hear me?

You control your relationship with God in the way you worship. You decide the status of your relationship or if you believe it at all. You can worship in the simple act of wearing a religious medal or in your commitment to attending daily services. More important is how you worship God in your thoughts. God can create opportunities to inspire you, but God can't make you worship. Worship is your choice.

Worship is harmony. Whether it's holding hands dancing in a circle or a chorus joined in a single note, human beings in harmony create energy. Worship strengthens your bond to God's harmonic tone. Through worship, you find your place in the circle. You find completion. That's why you love it. It's spiritual unity expressed in life. Dancers moving to hot, disco rhythms, a cheerleading routine, soldiers marching on parade, and civilization itself are all examples of human beings showing the equality of their individuality in harmony with their decision to be one with God.

Religious services provide a sensible way to worship. You may not know how so you need help. The ceremonial process is a great way to do it. The call and response to a leader's prayer draws the congregation into the powerful unity of the final "Amen." Even if you miss the point of the prayer, you recognize your mumbled "Amen" shows your respect for God. The unifying power of worship joins in that single word.

You may find more meaning in your private meditations. You don't need a religion to tell you how to pray. It helps, but with a clear conscience you can create your own ceremony. That's where ceremonies come from. You have an inspired thought that doing something a certain way demonstrates your respect for God. A ceremony is a mental aid to help you connect your life to God's Grace. It's not how you pray that matters. Your love is the connection.

Artifacts: Faith's Souvenirs

Your soul doesn't win by owning things. Your soul is measured by the love you create. God's power is in love, not in relics or the charms you wear. Relics are fascinating if you like history, but a loving thought is more powerful than any thing...no matter who it belonged to. Believing something has special powers applies human standards to spiritual values. That said, icons do serve an important purpose. They help remind you of God.

Can old bones and stained, yellowed pages hold the energy of a dead saint? I think they can. Is it right to revere those objects? To a degree, yes. A remnant of a soul's energy can rub off on a relic the same way your energy attaches itself to the things you own. Do you possess God's holy power to do with what you wish when you own those things? No. You possess God's holiness when you esteem love. You wield that power with an open heart, not your jubilance over a piece of wood you believe touched someone revered as holy. If it's power you want, it's in the wisdom of the prophets not some mojo you wear around your neck with a lock of their hair. God doesn't dance because you think owning a religious object gives you powers. The beauty of a religious object is its purpose, to focus your attention on God. How often have you used a religious symbol as jewelry instead of a symbol of your faith? Too often.

Proving God's existence to someone who only trusts science is impossible. The evidence isn't definite. Science's questioning begins with theories...reasonable guesses. But faith doesn't lend itself to mathematical proofs. Faith is anecdotal. It's in the stories of those who've experienced it. So what do you measure? Scientists seek answers in the physics they understand. Every generation's scientists invent machines to measure life's finer energies. They find clues but they can't agree on a meaning. They should try to measure love. Unfortunately, for scientists, love is measured by faith. You can measure the intensity of your beliefs by your body's reactions, but where's the meter for trust?

You live with a need for food and shelter. Your spirituality is the same. You have a need to feed your soul with love. There's nothing wrong with physical representations of faith as long as they support your spiritual values. Spiritual values are your life's work. It's easy to think a religious object could be the key that unlocks your spirituality. It's a reasonable step when you're learning your faith. You know how a key works. The real key is knowing that love creates your life. Mysteries of the past are a fun distraction. Faith takes your effort today. Wearing the team colors may support you, but God's community asks you to trust love. Religious icons don't protect you from vampires. Love protects you from vampires.

I forgive you.

You deserve a second chance or, really, as many chances as you need. With God, you're not allowed to fail. You choose the people you want in your life. With self-respect, you can accept someone's character and tolerate their problems or end a relationship that troubles you. Forgiveness comes from love and self-respect, not from desperation.

God's forgiveness is absolute because you're part of God's plan. You have free will because God wants to see what you do with it. God

131

learns from you. Through love you're connected to everything. You're independent in consciousness yet whole with the Universe. You're never separate so you're always forgiven, the same way you forgive yourself. You'll never be abandoned no matter what you do. You're a catalyst for God's growth, and you know how hard growing up can be.

God knows this and forgives you. God says, "Learn from what happened and do better next time." Even animals test their environment then adjust to improve their chance of survival like when a fox retreats from a porcupine on their second encounter. Like any good teacher, God tests you, prods you, stumps you, inspires you, fails you, rewards you, leaves you back, or skips you ahead. When things are too much, God's forgiveness comforts you. When things are too easy, God's forgiveness challenges you. God forgives your complacency too.

God forgives you when you're lost in selfishness. God knows how overwhelming life can be, how you might look for relief wherever you can. Your realization of love means everything to God. Your thoughts matter. In God's unwavering attentiveness are the unseen mercies God surrounds you with each day. You're forgiven your confusion so every thought you have is a chance to succeed.

Life is stressful and fears come up. There are times you're impatient and wish you could chuck the whole thing. You feel inadequate, disappointed in your lack of achievement. You get angry at life and afraid what your mistakes portend for the future. It's part of the game so God forgives you. Take comfort knowing whatever you do in faith, God forgives you. Actually, what you do blindly and selfishly God forgives you too. But forgiveness isn't a free ride where you can do anything you want with impunity. Still, you'll always have another chance to do better. If you don't mind having the same problem again and again, it won't mean much. Pay attention if you want to move forward though. God's forgiveness supports you but it can't do it for you.

Receiving God's Love with Grace

Accepting God's love closes the circle and completes your relationship with God. You invigorate it by forgiving God for your trials. The pain in your challenges recedes. God's Grace and your gratitude become one. The same as the whirlwind in the eye of a hurricane, your power increases. The parts disappear to become one gigantic storm. The circulation has no end. Giving and receiving is a cycle. Love's gift is your creative power. The more you give, the more you have.

It's like the saying from the Bible about careless behavior, "Sow the wind and reap the whirlwind." Only this whirlwind is positive. Don't be afraid when love finds you. It's a blessing you can handle. Put your trust in love and it'll show you how to work with it. It's not a deficiency to feel love. It's a blessing. Any time you feel love, you're doing something right. Love reaches out from the fog of life's chaos and invites you to join the miracle of God's unity. It doesn't take sides. A circle has no sides, only continuity accelerating to perfection. The faster it goes, the stronger it gets. And your love feeds it.

So feed it. Trust it. Enjoy it. Love is there for you. It's your choice to let it in. The walls you build are an illusion of protection. As you resist life's pressures you might see everything as a threat...including love. Love is your rescuer. People lie about love because love is true. The meaning of love is caring. You see it when you're honest with yourself and take off the psychic armor you wear to deal with life's questions. It's common in social situations to cling to images you think are successful. But no one can save you from yourself. Don't blame others if you're afraid you won't be loved. It's up to you to love yourself.

You're mixed up if you think you don't deserve love. It comes from denying yourself. You judge yourself unworthy instead of appreciating the magnificent soul you are. Life is a sow-and-reap process. You put something in and take something out. You work and get your reward. So love's gift is confusing. You may think it's a debt you owe. But you don't have to prove anything to anyone. You deserve love. It's who you are. You deserve the joy in others when they love you. And you deserve God's joy when God loves you.

Love doesn't come to you empty-handed. It brings you what you want in your heart. That's the meaning of Christmas, a special time to honor giving and receiving. Christmas gifts represent God's love. When you give St. Nicholas your wish list, "Granted!" is Santa's reply. "Granted." is God's reply to your desire to share your love. "It's better to give than receive." Well, it may not be better, but it's certainly as good.

Peace in Action

Peace comes from your desire for it. It doesn't just happen. It's your attitude towards love. Love gives you peace. It's an action. It's not the absence of anxiety. It's your love finding the love in others.

Peace needs your permission. Peace is your belief that you have what you want. It's loving your life. That's why peace is represented by beachside sunsets, pretty towns with birds chirping, and people walking around smiling. Peace is comfortable. Peace represents love's success enjoying the life you want, whether it's dancing in a ballet or riding herd on a cattle ranch. Peace isn't life without effort. Peace is your balance with Creation.

It's common to know peace as "rest." "Rest in peace." the saying goes, your last words to those who've passed on. No more life, no more strife, the end of all conflict. "Peace on earth. Good will to men." is the sentiment of the holiday season and your respect for God's love. Life's challenging, but if you can find your freedom despite your problems you've found your peace. Peace isn't your outer world. It's your inner world. No place has so much beauty that you can't be miserable there. And no place has so much misery that love can't make it beautiful again, at least in a moment of peace.

Peace is elusive but you can sense it. So how do you make it part of your life? You reward yourself with situations that make you happy. You love yourself. Peace is loving life, loving others, and damning the problems, not the other souls trying to find their own peace. Peace is love in action, not your perpetual creativity satisfying you for

134

a moment until some new distraction comes along. Peace is your work. Nibble at it when you're able. Grab it in chunks when you can. If you're greedy for anything, be greedy for peace.

The Last One on Earth

You probably know about the 144,000 souls mentioned in the Bible's Book of Revelations. They seem to be the holiest souls, the ones to be saved when the world ends. But what if these souls weren't the holiest? What if they were simply ushers whose job is to guide the Earth's souls to the next step when God's purpose for this world ends? It's certainly a respectable job, but it wouldn't make you better than anyone else. What if it wasn't 144,000? What if it was a million? Who knows? If you believe it, anyone who loves God would want to be part of this group. And so do I.

Here's how I see the end of the world. The million souls escorting those who were once human beings are lined up single file. At the end of the million, the last one in line is me. No problem. The first one steps up, gets assigned a few million souls, gathers them up, and leaves. This happens all day. A hundred thousand souls, five hundred thousand, a million, two million, no special amount, and one by one the ushering souls take their flock away. Everything looks good. Then they come to the end of the line where I am. There are millions of souls left so I figure they'll split them up between me and the soul in front of me. Surprise. The soul in front of me cleans the slate and takes every last soul off the planet. Now all the soul ushers are gone and all those who were once human beings are gone. There I am, standing alone, the last one on Earth.

I'm surprised but not upset. I think to myself, "Okaaay?" I look around. The world has a flat, barren look to it, no vegetation. I keep thinking, "What's going on?" All of a sudden, I turn to my left and there, about twenty feet away, is God sitting on a rock staring at me. "Hey, kid." God says to me. "Hey, boss." I reply. "Well, that's about it." "Yes, Mark, that's about it." Silence. Then God says to me, "Mark, I'd like you to do something for me." "Sure, boss. Whatever you need." Then God says, "I'd like you to tidy up a bit then meet us back in Paradise." "Okay." I say. Then God gets up, but just before leaving God turns to me and says, "One more thing Mark, don't take too long. We're going to be waiting for you." What's the moral of this story? *Everyone matters.* No one is without God's love and no one gets left behind. That's my job.

Chapter 7
Here or There: The Opposites

Mature at 40

I got older but I didn't mature till I was 40. It was at the end of my first marriage. I finally had a sense of responsibility. I realized my life was up to me. I realized other people depended on me. I remarried and had a daughter when I was 43. Maturing is the best part of having children. Parenting teaches you a lot about yourself but it takes time. It forces you to grow up and take care of your family. It forces you to be a leader no matter what age you are. Your children grow up and you grow with them.

Maturity is about timing and transformation. It's about taking the right step at the right time. It's preparing for your next step and making sure it's in the right order. You have to know arithmetic before you do algebra. Everyone has a personal curriculum about what they should learn. It's a process that builds on itself. Without that base, it's a fantasy. Being at the right place at the right time isn't luck. It's maturity. It just took me longer to get there.

Maturity teaches you patience, that rushing doesn't solve your problems. Attention solves your problems...and faith. Patience helps you find the best solution. It looks for durable solutions when you want something to last but doesn't challenge a temporary solution if that's all you need. It still expects an answer. You can't throw stuff in the back of your truck then speed around a corner and not expect

137

things to go flying out. Maturity tells you what to expect. Maturity taught me not to fool myself with exhausted images of my ability. A weak image is destined to fail. Strength gives you a chance. That's maturity.

Opposites: The Duality of the Universe

The confusion starts because you think you're alive, not realizing you're the soul you are. This isn't a problem. It's designed that way. This dynamic creates conflicts that create opportunities for your choices. That's your purpose, creating alternative values to choose from. That's what interests God. That's how God explores itself. Your creativity is God's gift. Variety is life's gift. Your values for love come from your soul. Your values for survival come from your life. How you integrate these two form the complexities of "right and wrong" because you're always trying to figure the best thing to do.

Your fears tell you life is everything. Your soul tells you love is everything. This is the paradox that your choices serve two goals. The solution is your happiness. You'd love to have a supernatural awakening that explains everything. Religion's answer to the absence of a defining experience is tradition. Religious traditions are a bridge between your body and soul. You can't sacrifice your spiritual values to possess everything you believe defines success. Neither is it reasonable to ignore your material responsibilities to spend your life alone in a monastery. Harmony is your goal. Like an air traffic controller managing dozens of planes, your job is to coordinate your priorities so they all succeed.

"Every action has an equal and opposite reaction." You learned that in grade school. Universal energy is balanced. The "balance of nature" explains how the environment adjusts to its changes. Water flows and the ground beneath it wears away or the water spreads out. Whenever energy moves, there's a counteraction to balance it. Balance isn't an opposite reaction. It's an equalizing force. The value is how it aligns with your plan. Your car wears down but your attention to maintenance is the counterforce that keeps it reliable. Or the thoughtless cutting down of trees to build houses can allow a hillside to erode letting rainwater cause mudslides that destroy the houses below.

Balance is cooperation. It could mean shifting your weight to make carrying your suitcase easier or amending a bill in Congress to satisfy everyone enough to pass it. When there's something you want, you adjust to accommodate it. It's how the shape of an airplane wing controls the pressure of the air flowing over it to make the plane fly. You create a personal balance in how you shape your character to achieve your goals and love yourself.

Social Balance

Social balance is a system of agreements that promote common interests...civilization. Social integration addresses common needs and assets. A healthy social order is knowing your needs are satisfied. Sharing the benefits creates the balance. Social balance extends from its core philosophy to distribute its resources fairly. Taxes are collected, water plants built, and everyone has clean water. It seems simple but with so many opinions, agreeing to the details is challenging. Where will the plant be built? Who'll pay for it? Who gets the water first? You have to agree on things that are continuing conflicts long after the need is accepted. A healthy society is built on compromises that treat everyone's needs equally.

Compromise isn't as simple as "Let's split it in half." Society has individual interests that constantly change. Social compromise is more than one decision. It's a series of interlocking agreements that create a policy. For everyone's interests to be respected, certain things are included while others are sacrificed for the overall good. As things develop, you might reconsider and change the policy later. Civilization's balance is the most exquisite juggling act this side of Creation. It's your personal values expanded to accommodate national and international interests. There's plenty to point your finger at and say, "That's wrong. That can't be fair." because your nature is always pointing towards unity.

From wandering nomads to the city-states that became today's modern nations, with regional interest organizations, international commerce agreements, national security pacts, world disease and disaster relief, and even a United Nations to address national conflicts, human beings continually strive for a balance that serves everyone. The most chaotic social environment is balanced by the love of the human beings who live there. You may want to erase your enemy from the face of the Earth, but you can't erase the social challenge of life and the questions only love answers. When part of the human race subjugates another, it upsets the balance. All it can do is create an artificial equilibrium maintained by the force of oppression. The Universe's inclination for balance presses against anything opposing it, especially fear and greed. Balance will eventually win out. The challenge to the solidarity of living souls resolves itself in cooperation. Cooperation through negotiation, fairness, and agreement is civilization's balance...and its peace.

Past generations faced their destruction to resist the imperialism that brought the world together. Today, unification through violence is gradually being replaced by expanding social benefits. The media is today's battlefield. The internet makes everyone a player. Humanity has matured. Love has evolved. And faith proves that balance is reliable.

Life and Death

Your birth thrusts you into conflict. You breathe or you die. You immediately know you're being challenged. You see dead animals in the street, shriveled plants on the kitchen counter, and you kill bugs without remorse. You understand life and death. Things are alive, and then they die and disappear. You understand, "Life is opportunity. Death is a sad end where people wear black and cry." You don't think much about it till you're threatened. You joke about it. You see it on TV. There's too much to do and no way to make your life last a day longer. Do you have a choice? Here's the thing. "Do you think anyone gets born or dies without God signing off on it?" Is your death negotiable? Yes. God is reasonable and would accept a fair bargain. But you don't negotiate it, your soul does.

You know when you're alive. For your soul, your demise is the final chapter in you being a human being. You do your best to handle life's paradoxes. Hopefully, you learn about love. That's a good life.

Breathing alone doesn't make a good life. You have to give value to each breath. What's important is how you use love to answer your questions. Somehow you survive. But when you judge your survival through love, God blesses you with wisdom.

God's energy is its awareness. It could be as a creative human being or as a tree aligned with its purpose to shelter the flora and fauna beneath it. Whether it's an opossum on its nighttime prowl or a rosebud opening to the morning sun, life is a process. Its balance is its cycles. It's a wonder how the variety of species repeat themselves so regularly. In the genes of plants and animals is the pattern that gives them their direction. They follow God's vision of what they should be. God influences you the same way. Your pattern is love, consciousness, and God calling you to explore your existence.

There is no end. Every species explores its cycles in succeeding generations. When things change, for whatever reason, its balance is challenged. So it adapts to it. It equalizes its current features with its new features. Change creates a new balance that grows wiser as God evolves. That's the plan. Change challenges you. It presents moral questions like, "Is it right to allow a species to go extinct or is it better to eliminate a deadly virus forever? Is there some benefit you're missing?" "Where human rights clash with natural rights, which are the priority?" Your God-given creativity is meant to help you answer these questions. You can and you must.

Nature

Nature is all the processes of the material world. It creates energy by consuming itself and transforms that energy into the world you know. That energy is your reality. But it never leaves its psychic roots. Nature and spirit are always connected. This is the nature you know, plants exploring their surroundings, animals probing the world with their inquisitiveness, and the elemental world investigating nature over time. Then there's you, trying to figure out how to make things better.

Everything uses its unique features to find support for its survival. Everything reacts to the pressure of existence as the push-pull of atomic energy keeps its engine running. That's nature. Beehives, moss, dust storms, and the endless alternatives form God's questions. You and Creation test your design; adapting and evolving. You compete, compromise, and contribute as you discover new answers to nature's eternally intriguing questions.

There's a constant competition for resources. It's about as weird a system as you can get. Nature succeeds by consuming itself. The strange thing is after all this consumption there's more of it, not less. Nature thrives by respecting its balance. It grows as long as its renewal outpaces its consumption. Nature knows this. The wildcard is human beings. Human beings' creativity can consume faster than nature's ability to keep up. So you have to decide if the short-term benefits are worth the long-term costs to the environment. Can the costs be mitigated to guarantee those resources will be there in the future? Can over-fishing and pollution be managed so we always have healthy fish to eat and safe waste disposal systems that respect keeping nature's miracle in balance?

Gender Balance

Propagation recycles life. By themselves, male and female energies are limited. Mating brings them together to recreate themselves. They join to create new individuals who possess the fertility to take their turn and mate again. This cycle keeps nature connected in the same way your relatives connect you to your past and future. The nature of fertility is life's desire to exist by balancing its male and female energies in a union that maintains Creation's mandate to endlessly explore itself through re-creation.

Creation doesn't end. It matures. Male and female energies join with the hope to create something better. No matter what image you have of your perfect mate, you connect with them through your maturity. While a peacock tries to attract a mate with its bold display of feathers, that doesn't mean it'll be successful. Creation knows what it needs and accepts fulfillment when it's in its best interests.

Nature is life's balance. Love is God's balance. Nature serves your human cycle in the same way love serves your soul's cycle. It creates order. It's a strange miracle. So many relationships. You'd think it should collapse but it doesn't. It adjusts...guided by God's cosmic gyroscope. It moves with the flow or resists it. The forces always balance but it may not be a peaceful balance. When the balance is disrupted, it may not return to its original shape. It respects equilibrium, not repetition. At the heart of the miracle is you, a human being. So if you want something, it's important to find a balance you can live with.

Balance is happiness, the successful complement of your male and female energies. You have both because love includes both. You can't avoid it because you disagree. You either include it in your harmony or you substitute a belief you can trust as long as you support it. Love is the real harmony. It balances on its own support. Without love, there is no balance. Love connects Creation and cares for every part of it. Everything cooperates so every part can succeed. When you open your heart, the barriers between energies disappear and love becomes whole again.

Marriage: The Process of Homogenization

Marriage has evolved. Old, established cultures are engaging new concepts of gender equality. Same-sex marriage proponents are successfully fighting for acceptance. In third world countries, freedom and technology are giving women their rightful say after millennia of male domination. In a growing number of places women are finding they can choose how they live and still honor their traditions. Mature attitudes are confronting ancient beliefs whose purpose has run its course. But it's a process that doesn't reflect everyone's opinion so "honor killings" still jar you when you read how a family killed their own children out of obedience to some ancient ritual. Even propagation has a new meaning with in vitro fertilization, advances in modern birth control, and surrogate parenting finding their niche in society. Today, it's easier than ever to have the marriage you want.

More than just making more people, there's a social side to marriage. The balance of male/female energies meets in the wedded couple. Marriage is their commitment to society as a couple. They create a family, whether it's the spouses alone or together with their children. The social balance is families working together. It joins the mating aspect of couples with the social aspect of a community. Marriage is the bond of social integrity; individuals who commit to each other, to their families, and to their community. Like a friendship or business partnership, it needs agreement. It needs sincerity.

What if you aren't married? Does that put you out of balance? That's what society's exploring now. More men and women are putting off having families till their careers are settled. More people are divorcing at a younger age creating single parent families. The freedom created by technology and advancements in social justice allow women to make their own living without depending on a marriage for support. There's a price though. The integrity of the supportive family is being challenged. The internet is replacing family elders in providing guidance to the next generation. But it's the media's commercial version. It's strangers with their own agenda. Today people know more but have less experience. Love is missing and maturity's not keeping pace. Freedom takes responsibility. New values are appearing and you have to trust God's love will guide it.

The balance in marriage is respect and support. Love is expressed through caring and sharing. Without marriage, social groups take its place. It can be your friends, family, or a support group that addresses your special needs, from spiritual responsibility to how to find a mate. A mate satisfies an essential part of yourself, your desire to share your privacy. You may not have someone to call your "other half" right now. You may not want it. You do want caring people in your life whether it's a best friend or your golf buddies. In time, you'll find your mate. They're looking for you now.

The Nuclear Family

The parent/child balance finds love in commitment. It's not balanced like a counterweighted scale. The changing roles of parent and child balance like a glass of water in a moving car constantly seeking a stable level against the motion of the car. It's a balance of maturing personalities taking responsibility and yielding responsibility as the situation demands. It requires both to seek their own fulfillment while they respect the balance in supporting each other. As each one matures, they adjust their dependence on each other always aiming at a constant level of love.

A parent teaches their child self-reliance and self-respect, the "golden rule." But even when life's possibilities are predictable, you can't guarantee how they'll show up. The human plight is; with all life's chaos you're a bundle of chaos yourself. A good parent understands the first lesson is that you create the world you live in. Being involved in life, like doing your chores and getting good grades, creates opportunities while avoiding things because it takes work stalls opportunities. The lessons you teach are the tools that answer your children's questions about how the world works. They're the skills that teach your children confidence and how to use their common sense.

Confidence is a balance of your self-respect and your respect for everything else. It's your belief in yourself that you can weigh them successfully with values flexible enough to meet any situation. Confidence is fair. It trusts you to decide what you need and what you don't. It's your self-control as you work within life's limits. It's your faith in God and trust in life. It's your God-given right to express yourself despite the opposition.

As a parent you teach your children to respect everything. But children feel their freedom and want to do whatever they want. Running carefree through a parking lot is fun, but it's also dangerous because other people use the parking lot too and moving cars are never safe to be around. Caution is the balance between respect for your freedom and respect for the things you don't know about, like that car coming around the corner too fast. You learned, "Look both ways before you cross." Your parents wanted you to be safe. They wanted you to learn that your confidence balances on your cautions.

Self-Love for Everyone

All positive relationships start with self-love. Before you can care about anyone, you first have to care about yourself. You first have to dignify your own interests. A loving relationship supports your dreams. Like the saying goes, "One hand washes the other and both hands wash the face." Mutual respect creates balance. You don't accept anything your common sense tells you is unfair. Life's a handful. Love is how you handle it. Love takes many forms, but it's always fair to those who share it.

You work with love but it's not easy. Where you draw the line between your interests and someone else's is the task. Most guidance is casual concern pointing you in some direction and saying "Go!" But how? It takes confidence and the realization that you don't know how. Fear is the six hundred pound gorilla...that if you don't do it right you'll lose everything. When you face a conflict, God reminds you to trust love. Love takes you by the hand and shows you how. If you love yourself, fear's defenses have no use to you.

What about others? Where does everyone's self-love find a unified balance? God's kindness is the balance, not self-interest at another's expense. Self-interest is your absolute responsibility but love's connection requires that you cooperate with others. There's peace in agreements. There's unity. Compromise creates the social balance. It's as simple as changing a meeting time to be more convenient for everyone or as unstable as a new partnership. You're a social being. You have to get along with others. Compromise shows that you can love yourself, care about others, and trust love to protect you.

Friends, Acquaintances, Enemies, & Strangers

Safety comes first. It's easy when you're dealing with someone you don't know. You're cautious. Situations are predictable and barring an unusual circumstance you know whether you're safe or not. Bridges fall down, but it's so rare you needn't concern yourself with it. People are different. People are unpredictable. Even the most reliable person can fall victim to a mood. When emotions come up, a person can act uncharacteristically and surprise your defenses. So who do you trust? You trust yourself and those who love you. Together you can do anything.

Friends give you balance. You find a common ground with those you trust. It could be a shared interest or, for whatever reason, you care about each other. You want them to succeed. Then there are your enemies. It's unusual to have such animosity that you'd call someone an enemy, but it happens. Unfairness, real or perceived, creates enemies. Creation is fair so being an enemy conflicts with self-love. It comes from self-hatred. It grows from misery and an inability to heal it. It tries to balance itself by striking out against what it believes confines it. Though its power is false, its presence is real and you still have to deal with it.

Who's your enemy? Is it someone competing with you at work or maybe it's that thug on the corner? It could be the crazy leader of a country halfway around the world or is it that stranger walking toward you? You have to make judgments about your welfare. You respect the social justice system to create fairness when you have a conflict with your neighbor. Whether it's a complex copyright argument or someone parking on your grass, justice's intention is to create fairness. It has many sides but just one answer...the establishment of legitimate rights. You're not alone when you face an enemy. Civilization protects you from enemies so the social system can prosper. Society is the priority because its stability serves everyone and enemies serve no one.

Not everyone thinks you're a gold coin, but you still have to get along with them. Do you know the names of all your neighbors? Most people mind their own business, but when a disaster strikes neighbors pull together to make sure everyone's safe. Safety is the balance of society, whether it's safety from criminals, a storm, or an economic downturn. You trust your acquaintances will find that cooperation serves everyone. Until then, protect yourself from enemies and surround yourself with friends. Strangers, though, represent uncertainty. At the same time, they represent hope. Common sense supports your hopes. It trusts love even in a mystery.

Confused, and you know it.

Balance comes from knowing what you're doing. Confusion is dangerous. When you can't identify a problem you feel vulnerable. Everyone likes a mystery, thrilled by the uncertainty. You want to know how you'll succeed. That's what sports are about, defeating the unknown. But the most experienced skydiver still checks their chute before jumping. Respecting your circumstances is the first challenge.

Your job gives you balance. Good relationships give you balance. Your hobbies give you balance. Balance is reliability. Your routines provide balance because you trust the objectives of those routines; money to pay your bills, love's support, and things that make your life fun. Life is the adult version of playing on a teeter-totter. While your routines are stable, you expect them to change. When your life is steady more than a moment, you feel successful and get bored like any child would. Your creative nature is ambitious. You want to know what new thing a change could show you.

When things go bad, you make them right. When things go good, you make them better. When you're confused, you look for what makes sense. Sometimes your confusion is too much. There are so many interconnected responsibilities. The accountant needs the car mechanic who needs the singer who needs the politician. It's endless. That's why you have questions. Answering questions is the job of your creativity. It helps you develop clarity. Clarity gives you certainty. Certainty grows your confidence. Confidence inspires your faith. And faith becomes your joy. Just accept that God wants you to love your life.

Doubts, Curiosity, Answers, & Acceptance

Doubts are disorienting. They allow too many possibilities and too many needless questions. You're still obliged to explore them if you think they affect you. Until you replace them with confident conclusions, you won't be comfortable. Acceptance, even when it's mistaken, is comforting. Ignorance is bliss but doubt is stress. Curiosity is its balance. It's fascinating as long as you feel safe. You'd even sacrifice some safety to answer your curiosity like when you poke your head in a cave to see what's there. From scuba diving to getting married, you're never without your sense of wonder. Questioning things is who you are. You thrive on it. There's nothing more basic than wanting to know more.

Uncertainties are distracting. They force you to stop what you're doing till you're sure. Some doubts will never be a problem even if the worst thing happens. Others could be dangerous and should be dealt with immediately so you know where you stand. Will that old ladder still hold your weight? You may not solve your doubts easily, but respecting your priorities will help you balance them sensibly.

Knowing the right answer is the most comforting thought in the world. When you study for a test you feel confident. You know the material. Life is a constant test where you always need new answers. Your questions share the gift of preceding generations who asked the same questions you ask now. Their answers created the world you trust today. Self-trust balances on the details you depend on. Reality must support your beliefs for you to answer your questions correctly.

Curiosity ignites your creativity. You don't know how but you want to know. You're not in danger but you want to know if there is a danger. You can avoid a danger but you can't avoid the unknown. The unknown is curiosity's home. Curiosity may have killed the cat, but you can't live without it. Really, neither could the cat. Curiosity inspires your creativity. It's God's way of wanting to know more. Wanting to know more is the secret that keeps God evolving.

Choices You Like and Choices You Don't

Your happiness is the proof. It's not about controlling the chaos in an acceptable way. If you have a goal, gauge your happiness by how you feel as you get close to it. For some, all it takes is a steady job, a loving spouse, and some good TV. Whatever it is, without it, you're unhappy. Unhappiness is imbalance. Your orderly nature won't allow it. You need a direction. You need a plan with a realistic schedule. Your plan is your first step from disorder to stability. All you have to do is follow it and not be discouraged by the obstacles. Obstacles are about timing, not ending.

One accomplishment may not bring you the success you want. Satisfaction comes from your accomplishments over time. Your satisfaction is in your ability to control your situation and make it what you want. Like an actor, you must control your emotions. If your emotions overpower your reason, it's easy to make decisions that benefit you but create new problems. In your excitement to have something, you might ignore other people. Everyone's entitled to their fair share. If you take their share, you're going to lose their support. Your satisfaction needs management. Spontaneity is fun, but satisfaction is a flow that should be treated with the same respect as paying your bills. You have to budget it to fit your situation.

You're responsible to yourself to eat, drink, and *be merry*. Though all souls are similar, you have your own personality to please. Everyone knows the difference between satisfaction and dissatisfaction. You need to know what it means to you. It doesn't mean you accept your dissatisfaction. It means you accept the process. You can hide bad feelings in a distraction but your true sense of happiness is always with you. So keep looking for it. Sometimes you hit it on your first try or maybe it's your hundredth. Hope fulfills your satisfaction because it believes one day you'll have it. Be satisfied with who you are, not where you are. There's more than the physical world to help you. There's a spiritual element in everything. Like shooting clay pigeons, even knocking down one is fun.

Control Your Confusion

Control takes skill. Fortunately it's a learned habit so you can do it. Confusion comes when you don't have a purpose so you cling to old habits. You march in lock-step with the frightened world, afraid to trust your creativity. It could be your inability to understand your relationships or not accepting responsibility when it puts you in a bad light. That's the meaning of confusion; relying on dissatisfying routines. It becomes important when you wake up and decide you want more. The counterweight to confusion is self-control. Control doesn't happen at the opposite end of confusion to balance it out. It works from the middle. Extremes cause confusion. From the middle you can guide it. That's what you have to learn, "Where is the middle?"

No one likes being confused. It makes you feel weak. But you don't have to be a genius to know right from wrong. You need an interest. When something interests you, you'll find a way to learn it. When you choose not be confused, you give yourself control. Anyone can be an expert on a slot machine. You push the button, the wheels spin, and you get your answer, win or lose. Everything but winning is predictable. Skill comes from your desire to change things in the specific way you want. Skill demands that you win every time. Skill puts you in the middle where you can see the value in everything.

Life is orderly confusion. That's its nature. It's predictable to a point. DNA sets each living thing on its pre-ordained path. Change happens continually but life's direction is clear. Physics guides nature within its limits. Natural conflicts resolve themselves in natural ways. Life consumes life and then is consumed itself. The weather finds conditions that create the balance to form a hurricane then disappears into sunny skies when the conditions change again. The confusion that comes from nature's chaos is logical. Excellent! That's what you're good at, being logical. You see balance where there doesn't seem to be any...because you know it's there. You just have to find it.

Control is your ability to do what's best for you. Confusion is uncertainty. No matter what your situation, if it isn't what you want it's uncertain. You create your certainty by engaging uncertainty and controlling it. If you're not sure you'll have time to eat, you bring a snack with you.

Carefree, Not Careless

Balance fulfills your responsibilities. It's good management. It ranges from being a good parent to being a good person. You know the unpredictable world you're up against. With all life's chaos, carefree is your freedom from doubt. All you have to do is answer one question, "What are you going to do with your freedom?"

Will you direct it or ignore it? Do you think it's just, "What will be will be." Is life always more work or could you win the lottery and make it all playtime? It's both so it needs your attention. Weekends aren't enough time to recover your strength, barely time to catch your breath. What your soul wants is the carefree freedom in a summer vacation or getting off early the day before a holiday. You want the weight of your routines lifted so you can feel your freedom. You want to put away the tough determination you need every day to survive. Carefree is the balance your soul needs to energize itself. It balances your work responsibilities with your soul's creativity so you can feel the freedom in God's love.

There's a part of you that wants to be carefree, even if it's just a moment raising your face to the sun to enjoy its warmth. You might like playing games. Games can be invigorating but they should be refreshing. Competition is great, but you have to leave its aggravations on the field. It's not a commitment. It doesn't affect your welfare. Freeing your cares means liberating your mind and trusting God. You can enjoy your freedom while you respect your responsibilities when you accept that one of your responsibilities is taking time to be carefree.

Being careless means ignoring your responsibilities and disrespecting yourself. Inconvenience and dislike are no excuse. Responsibilities are necessities not problems. God respects you for being responsible because there's love in caring. You may have a responsibility to a family member where your only reward is sharing God's love. That's fine. You live your whole life through God's love. Your freedom is in how well you accept your responsibilities, not how well you do at them.

Freedom, Work, And Happiness

Freedom gives you balance. It may not appear that you're free, but if you're satisfied it's through your own free will. In a job or marriage, you give away some of your freedom for the benefits of the relationship. Your freedom is intact in whatever you do willfully. When your freedom is constrained, then you feel pressure. Like exercise, some people like the workout as well as the benefits to their health and good looks. Others hate the process but enjoy looking good so they do it. If they could just snap their fingers, they'd rather do that than the work. Others prefer the ease in cosmetic surgery. They find freedom in achieving the result as fast as they can.

You might see your job as a sacrifice. You need the money but a job you don't like is a prison. You're somewhere you don't want to be, doing something you don't like to do, and you have to be there till someone says it's okay for you to go. You spend a lot of time working so it should be worth your effort. Your desire for balance is the freedom to do something else. Making money is a challenge for everyone. A solution that includes your freedom is the trick. That's what your creativity is for, to create a financial formula that balances your need for survival with your need for self-respect. That includes the courage to trade a reliable routine for an unproved opportunity.

Happiness is the balance in your heart. Pleasure is nature's comfort. There's a natural impulse to seek pleasure when you really want happiness. Pleasure is good, but reliance on pleasure is a weak substitute for happiness. You look for satisfaction in the things that give you pleasure: sex, eating, drinking, laughing, buying things, and playing games. Pleasure releases your inhibitions. Like the balance in happiness, it frees you from your problems for a while. You can respect the balance in pleasure by using it responsibly. Life lets you know when you've gone too far. Your body lets you know because it respects its well being. Just think, "Oh no, I've gained five pounds!" and "Oh my God, the credit card bill just came!" Or, "What do you mean, a baby?"

You're a center of the Universe. Its balance comes from you. You live among seeming random events. Your job is to use them. The world may be going six billion different ways and you might feel like you're going a hundred different ways, but the ebb and flow of balance move from a single point where your soul and humanity meet God's purpose so you can do your part supporting the Universe.

Laid Back or Outgoing

You get along with some people and not with others. Each personality has its own balance. Aggressive people like activities like skiing or entrepreneurial business projects. They enjoy the challenge. Their psychic make-up needs intense stimulation. Others enjoy less aggressive mental pursuits like the theater or reading, more thoughtful observers who enjoy exercising their minds safely. And there's every combination. Any activity can be pushed to its limit. The calm activity of a friendly chess game can become intense under the pressure of international competition where national pride and egos are at stake. While it's usually the activity that defines your personality, it's your attitude that empowers it.

You control your personal world. You have to feel secure with who you're with. It can be as relaxed as sitting by the pool with friends on a balmy day or as intense as the high-pitched camaraderie at a football game. Whatever it is, it has to satisfy you. It matters how you choose your friends. Your happiness depends on how well you mold your world to fit your personality.

Trusting folks is important because you're always meeting new people. It could be the church where you bring your family to worship. Your neighbors and co-workers draw you into groups by the circumstances that affect you all, like an increase in your property taxes or a change to your work schedule. To a degree you choose them, but a neighbor can move and who knows who your next neighbor will be, or workmate, or in-law? Relationships, like recipes, evolve when new personalities are added so ask yourself, "Would you benefit in knowing them? Do you really know who they are?"

Cooperation

Coordinating these personality types helps you keep your balance. Different points of view are useful tools. Other people's experiences expand your knowledge. No matter how confident you are, there's probably someone with a point of view you hadn't considered. It doesn't come from education, intelligence, or environment. It comes from God and the endless relationships God created between consciousness, life, and spirit. Anyone can have something worthwhile to say important enough for you to listen.

Know who you're working with. You share a purpose no matter how diverse your backgrounds are. The group must function as a team pulling in one direction. Things need to be organized and implemented. Each individual's skills create an advantage. Most people can do it all; size up a situation, find a solution, and take the right action. A group has the advantage of using whoever excels at the job. If a situation requires special skills, you may not be the perfect one to do it but a team can use the best in the group willing to do it.

There's a saying, "To a hammer, everything's a nail." But every problem isn't the same. Asserting yourself may solve your immediate problem, but it can leave bad blood if someone feels they weren't treated fairly. The next time you need them, they'll remember and you won't get what you want from them. Balance comes from respecting your differences. Every situation is new no matter how familiar. Don't get locked into old habits even if you decide the old solution is still best. Sometimes aggression is the key. Sometimes knowing the details works better. Or it may be a sympathetic attitude that seals the deal. Circumstances change. Attitudes change. You project balance by using what's appropriate at the time.

You need everyone's attention. When everyone contributes, everyone benefits. When everyone focuses on the same goal, that common goal eliminates their differences. It's like getting your tires checked so they don't wear out prematurely. You make regular adjustments to equalize the pressures. It's never fix things once and done. Problems repeat themselves. Every team works the same way, whether it's the cast of a Broadway play or a pit crew changing tires at Daytona. Cooperation compensates for individual weaknesses to project the full power of the team.

Up or Down, This or That, Ad Infinitum

Balance creates opportunity because whatever bad thing happens its opposite always exists. You can strive for success because you know it's there. Creation's purpose is to explore itself. However difficult God made your choices, hopefully you embrace them. Life is about applying love to your choices. You thrive on the mountains you climb. Your adventure began in Spirit long before you first mixed finger paints in those bold, satisfying swirls.

There's balance in variety because there's so much of it. With a small selection it's easy for one thing to dominate. As the largest statistical sample possible, Creation creates a structure that supports every consideration. It allows every concept the freedom to pursue its end until it becomes imbalanced to the point God reins it in again. Love has no opposition. Love is perfect balance. When you go exploring, whether it's looking for a job or seeking a mate, it's important to know variety is your support until you find your balance. And you'll know it when you love it.

Normal differences you accept. It's extremes that bother you, like the monster in a horror movie. If something's far away, it's easy to accept. When something's close, then you feel it. It means you're right where you should be. People's differences blend in society. Men, women, races, generations, cultures, personalities, religions and every mix demonstrate that you're only limited by your willingness to find a balance that empowers love.

You and Creation form a balance that allows you both your freedom while still combined in a single concept. You're a willing participant. You're an explorer. Specifically who you are doesn't matter. Love joins all journeys together.

Here or There

"Here or there?" is a question of opposites. A better way to describe it is, "Here or where else?" That includes where you are now and every other place possible you could be. You're choosing between unknowns so "Where?" requires good judgment. When you limit yourself to two or three choices, it's easy. You can examine each one without the details overwhelming you. When you're deciding where to move a chair it's simple, but if you're considering which career is best for you then your options cover every aspect of the human experience. "Here" is the easy part. The unlimited "Where else?" requires that you carefully question yourself because you have to live with the answer.

Whether it's love, money, or playing the guitar, your *satisfaction* is the same. Positive emotions translate into the things you like. Fate may effortlessly guide you. For most, and probably you, you have to work at it. You can play it safe and have normal relationships. Billions of people do. It's reasonable. You go to school. Get a job. Raise a family. That's the "Here." Society shows you a proven success. The "Where else?" might be a tale about someone who tried something new and succeeded, like the stories of the internet kings who quit school to go on and build successful businesses. Your heart knows what you want but life is a challenge. Trust God won't abandon you. There's nothing to gain in your doom. Somewhere on the road between "here and there" you have to choose what you like and expect God to be there.

"Here" isn't hard to balance. You know where you are. You balance the "Where else?" by being honest with yourself and being brave. Trust your common sense. Common sense and prayer are your tools. It's not a religious worship prayer as much as a staying-in-touch with God prayer. It's respecting God's plan will show you what you need. Your consciousness connects you to Creation. Expect it to be reasonable. A wheel will work the same way on Earth as it does on Mars...or anywhere else.

More or Less: The Endlessness of Opposites

Opposites complete each other, but they can clash and repel each other too. You control the contradictions by taking advantage of their individual traits. It's the same in a marriage or a treaty. Where forces repel each other, you have to adjust them from *all sides* to create the peace. You have to understand the features that create the balance *within* those interests, like the different factions in a political party. Individual interests must be addressed in the same way a stepchild adapts to a new parent. For whatever changes you make, something has to move to accommodate it. It means everyone benefits because balance is an alliance.

While anything can move you in a new direction, your strength is in keeping it balanced. You can take control and force yourself out of a stale situation to create a new balance that supports what you admire. Training does this to break old habits and create new ones, whether it's bodybuilding or improving your faith through affirmations.

Balance is real and you choose it. But an unnatural balance needs your attention. You may be a smoker and know it's bad for you but you like it or have trouble quitting. The question is can you create a balance that gives you comfort without the harmful effects of the cigarettes. Balance is self-control. Whether it's changing the ingredients in a recipe to accent a flavor or adding a new player to energize your team, working with opposites is a creative balance. Creativity means exploring different combinations. You balance these with your soul. The love in your soul is the equalizer. Love is your insurance that whatever balance you find fits neatly in the niche the Universe made for it.

Say Enough, Not When

Balance is having enough. You're comfortable when you have what you need, like good relationships and money to pay your bills. Just wanting "more" without any purpose like Edward G. Robinson's criminal character "Johnny Rocco" in the movie *Key Largo* is the fear of being impoverished. With that kind of thinking you can never have enough. And you can never enjoy the balance of having enough. You know what it means to be lonely or broke, or worse, without opportunities. Regardless of how much you have, it's threatening to feel you might miss having more.

Resources give you balance. Maybe it's a steady job or your good health. It could be a loving mate or trustworthy friends. Clear goals and a sense of responsibility give you balance. It's your courage and self-respect, your respect for others, and your love for Creation as you grow as a human being. It's your sense of accomplishment. Growth is your balance no matter how wobbly it is. You can never stray so far that God won't find you and set you straight again. Balance isn't a safe place where you hide from life. It's your trust in life.

Love will always be in balance. Love will always be enough. Your peace is knowing that in time you'll have what you want. You're empowered by your creativity, but your soul gives it direction and seeks love in everything you do. It's neither greedy from fright nor reticent from a false sense of unworthiness. It's carefree and trusting, like a child chasing a colored balloon. Every soul's peace is love. You realize it by wanting it, thinking about it, and recognizing that many people can't explain it. You create love by caring about others and trusting love to answer your questions. Don't worry if the things you do for love don't work. Like wood on a fire, your love fuels the power God uses to renew itself and create more love.

Healthy or Unhealthy: Diseases & Cures

Your natural balance is health. Since it's natural, it's easy to take it for granted. Even when you get ill, all you really want is to get back to where you can take your health for granted again. It's not stupidity. It's normal to want to be free of distractions so you can go happily about your life. Unfortunately, you can't avoid nature. The nature of your body is its functions are subject to disease and deteriorate with age and disuse. While durable, you have limits. Everyone's different in how strong their body is in resisting life's pressures, including the psychic stress that can overload your physical and psychological well-being resulting in textbooks full of disabling conditions.

Feeling good through the positive energy of your well-being is your balance. When you don't feel good, you'll do whatever you can to get well. You may have to decide on the value of taking a drug, long-term rest, or some medical procedure. You'll need to weigh the balance between the promise of relief and the possibility of discomforting side effects. Healing proves that health is your normal condition. You get better. You get your balance back. Natural forces will always affect you, as common as stepping halfway off a curb and twisting your ankle.

You accommodate health problems the best you can. You may have a genetic disposition to a disease or suffer an accident. Sometimes you subject yourself to contaminants if the only work you can get is at the local mine or chemical plant. Even when you know it's dangerous, you still need money to feed your kids. Under the pressure of modern society your psyche may be burdened by the compromises you make to survive. It can lead to burnout or the frustration in feeling trapped. To maintain your balance you might seek risky gratifications and fantasies to justify the paradox of doing things you don't like to survive. Once you feel you've achieved a level of balance, your soul may be conflicted when you realize you're doing things you know aren't good for you.

You bathe every day to feel clean and love yourself. Cleanliness is comforting. It's part of the balance that makes you feel good. Cleanliness inspires your attitude. It's a fresh start to whatever you're doing. In the same way, you clear your mind of negative thoughts by having a positive attitude. You bathe your concerns in patience, forgiveness, and love. Aside from the unique lessons in a severe illness, your daily health reflects your psychic balance. Illness isn't a punishment. It's an imbalance, an opportunity to rebuild. Never waste the lesson in an illness. There's a reason for everything and it's personal.

Comfort or Discomfort

Most people enjoy the same comforts, like sitting down after a long day, but personal comfort is the unique balance you choose. Some people like yoga. Others like swimming. Comfort is subjective. Your comfort may be in the simple pleasure of eating a hot dog while someone else needs a gourmet meal to find their comfort zone. You know what makes you uncomfortable too. You don't like being limited. That you learn early.

Your comfort needs attention. Comfort is having what you want the way you want it. You're the only one who can value what you want and accept what you have to do to get it. Acceptance is an important asset when it's your responsibility to make sure you're comfortable.

When you need help to be comfortable, it's different. That joins your agenda to someone else's and you have to satisfy them both. The key is reliability. You're comfortable when you're sure you'll get what you want. A steady job means you know you'll have money to make your car payment and a good marriage means you can count on your partner's support. Agreements aren't always successful but the potential is there. You might find someone you like in business while another is better at listening to your jokes. Your comfort comes when you find all the relationships that satisfy you.

Expected or Unexpected

You have expectations but results are unpredictable. You do your best to make your life reliable and find comfort in a peaceful balance. With courage, you start each day with the hope of doing well. Each moment you direct your progress, learn new things, and change your world to accommodate your balance. That's maturity. It's important to know the difference between what's valuable and what's just attractive. Life won't let you get too comfortable. It's not in God's interest to see you stagnate. Dependability is limited in God's eyes. God sees itself as the ultimate dependability. Balance is your belief that God can be trusted.

Your expectations rely on your questions. Questions are about possibilities. Creativity means there's no end to your possibilities. Even when you feel you're at the end of your rope, something can change to send you in a new direction. You may have to wait, but success has no schedule. As ideas dance through your head, you're living proof of the possibilities. You're not going to fly around the room, but you can go hang-gliding or float on your back in the ocean. You have alternatives. You have an idea of what you want. You control your expectations by asking more questions.

Expect to see love in everything. There's no opposite to it. Love is whole. Your soul feels it. All you can do is try to explain it. Your expectation of love encompasses every thought and emotion in the soul of Creation. In all life's chaos, love balances everything. It includes every loving sacrifice and every hateful thought. Love doesn't judge selfishness or charity. Love knows the difference but needs to experience it. As you improve your deficiencies, so does love. Whether it's your daily chores or your highest ambition, there's always something for love to learn. Your life reflects the nature of Creation. The difference is you work on your balance so Creation can question it.

Questions & Answers

Where's the balance between a question and its answer? When does the unknown become known? The balance of a question equates your doubts with your purpose. The answer may be important or not. Life exercises your creativity in the questions you ask. That's why you're naturally attracted to curiosities. Your soul is clear but life is a mystery. The question your soul asks is, "What affects me?" Then it matches love's values to nature's demands for the answer.

If love is the measure of life then your questions mark its gauge. Your questions reflect your spiritual momentum. Look at your thoughts. Always questions. "What's my situation?" "Where should I be?" "Can I use it?" "Is it worth it?" "What would be better?" You're constantly examining your values in relation to your options. It's an all-encompassing drive you don't even know you have. Yet, when you think about it, that's all you do, even in your dreams. It's God's creative process expressed through you. You're constantly asking questions and choosing the best answer. Your answers guide your future questions. The balance in your questions is being honest with yourself.

Sincerity means whether or not you have the right answer, or even the right question, you always want it to be right. Your balance comes from embracing the process. You question everything to see its value. You want to succeed so you keep asking questions. Everything in life is a mystery waiting to be answered even if you've done it a hundred times. Things change and you always want to be sure.

People are more or less fair but their values can clash. Then a decision has to be made as to what's fair between conflicting points of view. There's the image of the blindfolded Lady Justice, sword in hand, holding a balance scale weighing the truth. That's enough to respect humanity. The higher nature of human beings believes in equal opportunity. People prize fairness enough to create a system of justice in every culture. It could be a king, a council, or a system of laws and courts, but its purpose is the same...to achieve fairness. Whether you think it's karma or getting a fair shake, it's the answer to love's question, "What balance treats everyone fairly?"

Agree or Disagree

Your questions are the process. Your sincerity weighs the answers. Sincerity is only satisfied with the truth. If an answer proves incorrect then the balance shifts to your knowledge. Can you trust the source? Did the weatherman get the forecast wrong? Did your accountant make a mistake on your taxes? These can be honest mistakes. You can check everything and still miss something important. Things can be confusing when you rely on answers that are carelessly or intentionally misrepresented. Not everything happens as planned and the truth can be obscured.

162

When someone tells you something they know is wrong so you do something you wouldn't do if the information was different, it's a lie. You control the information you trust by using common sense. People naturally support their interests. You still expect them to be honest. You expect a fair trade. A trade can be for love, money, or anything. That's how you get by. You don't want your money squandered or your love ignored. You don't want to be cheated. You want the truth and a fair deal or maybe a little better for the bargain hunter.

Arguing the truth or agreeing to something you know is wrong is imbalanced and will eventually collapse. Stubbornness, doctrine, wishful-thinking, and bad advice all contribute to false beliefs. What was once true can change. Something can be true in some cases but not in others. If arguing provides a better understanding, like in a courtroom, then everyone benefits. Opposing views should be respected until an accurate understanding is achieved. It can be hard to accept the truth when it goes against your interests but it leaves you better off even if it's a burden. It's important to maintain a healthy debate in your mind. You can't go through life doubting everything. Your faith and sincerity are often the only tools you have.

Problems, Formulas, & Solutions

The balance between a problem and its solution is the change that makes it right. It takes the imbalance in uncertainty and produces a solution that makes it dependable. It might mean replacing a part that doesn't work or creating a new approach. You have to find the concept that solves your problem and helps you achieve what you want, just like you'd use a broom handle to extend your reach. The balance of the equation turns on that concept. You decide its function, whether it's choosing the right color eye shadow or steadying a crooked ladder.

It's an ongoing process so expect it to change. Foresight and common sense help but things don't always move predictably. You don't always get things right. You do your best but life is a challenge. Some are universal problems we all encounter. Others are personal to you. The essence of a difficulty is your inevitable success. Embrace your problems as steps to your goal. No matter how improbable it seems, your momentum keeps you balanced defying failure like the carnival motorcyclist challenging gravity in the "cage of death."

Your physical problems include your health, finances, relationships, and maturity…with details as long as your arm. It's harder to see your spiritual problems. They hide in the patterns of your life. You have to be interested and honest to see them. Spiritual problems test your belief that you can be a better person.

Solutions can be temporary, like carrying an umbrella when you expect it to rain. Sometimes that's all you need. A change does its work and you're done. You stabilized the situation and go on. If you're worried a problem might reoccur, now you know how to fix it. You're experienced. You don't have to guess. You just have to focus on what you already know.

Creating or Loving

Creativity finds balance in being appropriate. You can do wonderful things when you focus your creativity. It's always front and center. You wouldn't waste it daydreaming unless you enjoyed the beauty in your meandering thoughts. Your worst thoughts don't abuse it. Your values may be distorted but your creativity is always beautiful. You don't have to be smart. Like a good stretch, your creativity only wants you to be comfortable.

Your creativity balances on your attitude. It's the concept behind "It doesn't matter if you win or lose, it's how you play the game." The old saying is easy to laugh at when winning makes you feel good, but in eternity love is your bounty. How you play the game is about love. You have a relationship where you and God create in different ways, God complete looking inward while you look outward testing God's possibilities. Nature is God's creation. Your creativity has a responsibility to negotiate it through love. Creativity without love is hollow no matter how clever it is. When you give or receive love, it counts. You feed love in one end and more comes out the other side. That's the miracle.

Love is your spiritual nature. Always remember that. You're a loving person. Remember your kindnesses. Be grateful for the kindness you receive. Feel your gratitude. Reciprocate kindness even if it's only in your mind. When you send ten dollars to your favorite charity, don't rush to get it over with. Think about what you're doing and why. Attach love to each gift. It's the same for a corporate gift or the neighborhood kid selling candy to raise money for their school. Charitable thoughts amplify the love in your generosity.

Whole or Apart

The great wonder in Creation is the individualization of consciousness, wisdom split into infinite parts, whole and at the same time expressing their unlimited individuality. Contrary concepts existing together but not opposing each other. Instead, balancing each other's energy to create new opportunities. God's consciousness and Creation exist for each other. When you relate to anything, you're relating to God.

You do the opposite. You join things together to create a new purpose. It makes sense. When it rains, you know what's going to happen. Everything gets wet so you adjust for it. You wear a raincoat or stay indoors. Consciousness includes your ability to choose any result possible. Plants and animals have a degree of free will but you're special. God gave you imagination and the power to create in the same way God can. Creation pulled things apart. Your ability to "create" brings them together again in the endless ways you discover.

God's love is more than the world you can measure. It comes from Spirit, a more refined energy that's just as real. If everything is love then you can put that energy to work for you. Unadulterated by human desires, your kindness burns brilliantly. Your will releases it. Love is about values. Your exploration of love is why you're alive.

How do you control the Universe? If God makes everything happen, what chance do you have to change anything? Your job is to control parts of it. That's why you have free will. Whatever your inclination, love must be part of it if you want it to be worth anything. So God showed you the way. Love. You'll never run out of God's love. And creativity. God's given you your unlimited imagination. And for

165

survival, God's given you common sense. You have everything. So build something you love because building brings the parts together.

Us or Them: Taking Sides

Who's your friend? Who loves what you love? Who hates what you hate? The lines are drawn so you pick sides. But doesn't love make everyone a friend? Survival creates conflicts. Competition, whether it's for political power or to be first in line for this year's hottest toy can push you beyond what's fair to own it. Desperate extremes where your life or freedom are at risk you understand, but some people attack rivals out of low self-esteem as fistfights between sports fans attest.

There's fun in rivalries. Our team is better than yours. Our company is better than yours. Our country is better than yours. Then you point out whatever you think proves it. None of it matters. Picking sides is just another way to give your life value. You feel safe connecting to others with the same priorities. You have enough similarities to share your support. You can root for your hometown team or take pride in your company's products.

Relationships can sour when rivals become enemies with total disregard for each other's welfare. Love is ignored, replaced by an all consuming greed for victory. The only thing stopping a war is the psychic toll of intolerable suffering or there'd be nothing to slow it down. Good people get absorbed in war and it can take years to prove its uselessness. Eventually people tire and come to their senses to live in peace again. That's a battle of equals. The truth is big fish eat little fish and there's a history of powerful nations absorbing weaker ones. But then you're stepping on God's toes, destroying the beauty in God's diversity. God will always make things right as proved in the new identities of colonial nations forced to integrate the cultures of their former colonies. Sometimes social evolution needs a shake-up. As unpleasant as an unexpected change can be, progress results and new generations find opportunity in their freedom.

To get along with others you have to incorporate your differences with self-respect. With the internet, cell phones, and tomorrow's inventions, it won't be a village anymore; everyone will be your neighbor. It'll be hard to avoid. New rules on privacy are being developed. It means your self-respect will be more demanding than ever. This is the next step in human evolution. It means adjusting your beliefs to fit this new model. You don't have to like it. You have to respect it. And you have to be respected where you fit in. And, most of all, you have to trust God is guiding this amazing change and keep questioning it.

Good Luck, Bad Luck: Dame Fortune and the Vicissitudes of Life

Everything changes. Sometimes you change it. Sometimes it changes you. Sometimes change is a process that keeps repeating itself. Change isn't arbitrary. Things don't start as one thing and then go anywhere. They change with a purpose. The cause of many problems is that you don't accept it. So you build your house too close to the river and the river's flood cycle eventually inundates your home. You know the danger, but you risk it for the pleasure of living by the river.

A thrill is the risk in unexpected changes. Danger moves you to protect yourself. You might enjoy the thrill, whether it's riding a roller coaster or spying for the CIA. You take a chance every day driving sixty miles an hour down the highway and it feels perfectly safe. The benefit is great and the risk seems small. Then there are times you're sitting at a traffic light and the car behind you plows into you at twenty miles an hour. Things change that you can't control. More important are the changes you plan, like when you start a family or build a business. You risk your time and effort, *your life*, to do something worthwhile.

There's no punishment or exaltation in God's plan. Every day you do your best to work through it. God doesn't judge you for it. God guides you through it. This seems an easy way to explain away your failures when every day you're focused on success. But you don't fail on purpose. It's rare to have a life of only failure or success. It happens. Everything happens. Most lives are a checkerboard of joys and sorrows. Change teaches you things. Someone you love dies or maybe a new friend comes into your life. You can't avoid your fate.

You wouldn't want to. You may not want to look your age, but you wouldn't want any less maturity.

Vicissitudes are life's ups and downs, God's changes. Creation follows patterns that make these changes understandable. That's why you spend so much time questioning love. Love is your guide. Everything grows until it dies. I expect even the Earth will die in the eons ahead. Your timeframe is easier. Your purpose is to engage as many changes as you can stuff into a lifetime to increase God's understanding of Creation. You might think perfection is a safe place to hide but real perfection is change, even just thinking about it.

How do you control your luck? Having goals and working hard help but it's not everything. Beyond your goals is your belief. Beyond your belief is your fate. Beyond your fate is your love. Good luck comes from loving yourself with a positive attitude and knowing your purpose. That's your fortune, not any circumstance. It's your belief that whatever happens you can use it. Again, it's the old concept, "Every cloud has a silver lining." Don't fault it. Don't worship it. Don't give a situation any special importance. Deal with it. Expect good things. That's your luck.

Up, Down, Approved, Denied: The World of Opposites

Everything you know exists as an opposite; up or down, in or out, right or wrong, it's endless. Everything you experience has an opposite concept in reverse. Just as you'd raise or lower the volume on your radio to achieve a sound level you like, opposites have values you can choose. Increase the volume and the soft tones disappear while the loud ones are enhanced. You enjoy the beat of the drums better. Go too far and it hurts your ears. You work with opposites to create a useful balance. Change those forces and you create something new.

When the stem weakens with the increasing weight of the apple it can no longer support it and the apple falls to the ground. In life's constant commotion this repeats itself regularly. So how do you find your balance when everything keeps growing? Where action is the password, it must be in the activity itself. You do something. Action creates the balance. When you see something you think is incomplete, what you're really saying is it doesn't serve your purpose as much as its opposite would. It's having things a certain way. Everything you want has a formula for success. That's what you're looking for. Love's success is knowing what's missing.

Your purpose determines its opposite. If something isn't giving you what you want, do something that does. What if Creation just stopped? Would its energy disappear? Wouldn't you still have the opposite energy in stillness that eventually gets bored and starts creating again? Energy is aware. Awareness questions itself. You define Creation through your inquisitiveness. Whether it's chaotic or void, you can always do the opposite.

Yes or No

Red light, green light, stop or go; these are your first lessons. Do or don't? Yes or no? They question your state of mind, the balance of your well-being at the moment of decision when you ask yourself, "Could things be better?" Then you decide and your happiness weighs the result.

In nature, your choices decide your success, but with people, it's permission. Success with people comes from agreements and the balance you create with them. Negotiating the values of different features is how you make it work. You can organize a business deal where the details of different interests intersect perfectly so everyone makes money. Or you could take a romantic relationship a step closer to marriage when you trust each other enough to make a commitment and get engaged.

You're familiar with negotiations in business. Business is trade, something for something, so you want a good deal. Every day you trade solutions to your problems. It could be money, ideas, or time. When you buy gas or groceries, you're doing business. Your balance is your comfort with the purchase. Opposite sides meet to create something both can use. So see yourself in the other person's shoes, understand their needs, let love show you fairness, and be creative! Then everyone can say, "*Yes.*"

Dependence or Self-Reliance

The balance in cooperation doesn't have two sides. It has billions. But there aren't billions of personalities. In American politics the two main views are Democrat or Republican. In sales there are four basic personality types; driver, expressive, amiable, and analytical. There are twelve signs of the Zodiac to describe your personality by your time, date, and place of birth. After all the arguments the simple question is, "For or against?" No matter how many issues a government negotiates to keep its society running, it always comes down to evaluating the pros and cons and agreeing what to do.

There's always negotiation in government as different points of view present their interests in how governing policies affect them. Some want the government to do everything. They want their lives dictated so they can rely on the system. Others want minimal government. They feel too much government is a burden on their freedom. Most trust the middle road. It's human nature to want your freedom, but common sense shows you the benefits of compromise and working together. The reality is when a disaster strikes everyone looks to the government for help. A flood is too much to handle whatever your attitude is on self-reliance. Everyone has a time they need help.

How much freedom you're willing to surrender is up to you. You might like living at the end of a dead end street where no one can bother you or your house could be the local teen hangout. People who spend time together help each other. How much help you need depends on your circumstances. Do you like doing everything yourself or are you an invalid depending on others by no choice of your own. Just moving a couch is easier when two people do it. It may be your family, a friend, or your local town government. At some point you'll need help. There's always something you can't do yourself. It's good to have friends no matter how self-reliant you are. And the government helps too, even if it's just filling in potholes.

Solved or Unsolved

Existence is the balance of its parts. It includes the male-female balance where opposites attract to create energy in the same way a moving hammer strikes a stationary nail so the force created drives the nail forward. For any system to work, its opposites must be balanced. A hammer's glancing blow will bend the nail. The reason for organization is to coordinate the parts so they deliver the desired force. That's what you accomplish when you work with others to move that heavy couch you couldn't lift by yourself. That's the value in Creation as its limitless experiences help you define it.

Can you solve the mystery of your existence by understanding its opposites instead of seeking a single solution that eliminates all conflicts? Creation began by creating opposites. While the Universe may seem whole, it maintains its equilibrium by balancing the features of its individual energies. The elemental world is built on energy. Energy is God's consciousness. It started from a single force which expanded into its opposite...limitless materiality. God formed particles that built on each other then created you and your creativity to give them a purpose. God doesn't know why it exists. God examines itself through Creation, through you. Only God's love makes it whole, always incorporating its opposites.

A good example is the interaction of gears. It's opposing forces working together, rhythmically intersecting to transfer the energy and move the power forward. The interlocking teeth move in unison to focus the energy. This concept gives you control. It shows how you focus your own energy using the "gears" in your life, your opportunities. The seeming opposites of the material and spiritual worlds come together in love. Your thoughts energize an image that attracts the creation you want. Your creative thought is like steam condensing into water then becoming ice, then even denser on a cosmic level as it interacts with Creation. Your dream becomes real. Just love it. Through love you acknowledge God's purpose in it.

Love: The Peace in Differences

Though life seems chaotic, Creation connects it in perfect timing. Nothing is separate even with all its individuality. Creation is an entity. Regardless of its differences, love makes sense of it. Purpose is universal. Differences are the sweetness that makes it interesting. God's purpose is to give expression to its energy. Every creation is a microcosm of God's intent.

It's like sitting in an airplane staring out the window waiting to take off. You see the activity around you as the ground crew readies the plane, then you taxi down the runway and everything rushes by till the plane takes off and you're up in the air. Looking down you see the streets and highways, the patterns of the place. You understand more about it, its problems and opportunities. Then you rise so high all you can see is the sky and you're left alone with your own thoughts. You're so high all the hustle and bustle seem like a oneness where, unthreatened and alone, you can finally find your peace.

Things look different from a distance. When you see something far away it seems motionless, part of the background, but when you get closer you can see its individuality. It's like the twenty/twenty rule for car buffs. An old car looks great going twenty miles an hour from twenty feet away, but when you get close you can see its imperfections. In a universe of opposites the one neutrality is God because it includes love's opportunity in everything.

So where's your individuality? It's in your humanity and free will. It's in your imagination. It's in your likes and dislikes and your goals, or at least your desire to have them. It's in your thoughts and feelings. It's in your soul's purpose expressed through you. Your success is in how you align yourself with God's plan against the background of Creation. It doesn't need a detailed analysis. It's your attitude at the moment. When you develop a constant attitude of love, you'll find your peace everywhere.

Future or Former

Balancing opposites means using their energy in the same way judo takes the movement of a striking blow to send it off in a harmless direction. Conflict is avoided. Creation does this by using orbits to establish balance where opposites move around each other instead of crashing into each other or shooting off aimlessly. You see it in the stars and their orbiting planets and how atomic particles circle each other to create nature's elements. Opposing forces work together because Creation uses everything.

You control the present. Resolving the past and planning for the future occur in the present. You might worry about getting old, but age isn't the issue. The issue is attractiveness. You want the opposite sex to find you attractive. You want an employer to find you attractive. You want people to respect you. Age doesn't matter. You think it's important because it's material, something you can control with surgery and hair dye. Your character is what matters. You can take care of your looks and be attractive to strangers or take care of your character and be attractive to God. Or do both. But you have to decide if appearance alone will ever be enough to satisfy you?

Life recycles love. In a nuclear family you mature to when you can start your own family. From school to work, you become part of the community. You do that for years, then retire and hand the world over for a new generation to discover. They follow the pattern. The past, present, and future, like a spiral, are one continuous line. Everyone is born, grows up, dies, then orbiting like the planets leave their seeds for the next generation to nurture. Recycling love maintains life's balance as God's consciousness expands with the wonders each generation finds.

Chapter 8
Feeling, Knowing, & Being

Life is good training but you have to pay attention.

I enjoy improving myself. I like learning new things about myself. I like being better at what I already know. I have more self-control. I have greater emotional balance. I feel better about myself. I'm better at choosing my priorities. That's the tough part, because the right thing to do keeps changing with the situation. But I accept it as long as I can justify my sincerity.

I've worked on myself a long time. The alternative was my miserable existence. I'm never satisfied unless I'm truthful with myself. I may be wrong but I don't want to fool myself. Simple results aren't enough. Things have to be done right or I'll rearrange them till they are, even after the fact. The future builds on the right things you do today. That's why I wrote this book. I'm the kid who wants to do everything himself, not just receive the largesse of the Universe.

I pay attention without even thinking about it. It's natural for me. I'm fascinated by the way people think. I worked diligently to understand myself so now it's easier to understand others. It's obvious when someone's relying on a false attitude for their opinion. It's a matter of honesty and loving yourself. Self-love isn't judgmental. Self-love expects you to grow and be the child of God you are. The most embarrassing situation includes the seed of growing through it. If you see yourself as maturing, then everything in your life foreshadows you as a happy person. The humility that reflects the perfection in your soul grows in the richness of your experience.

Sincerity

Sincerity is your certainty that your goal is worth it. It's not correctness. It's perfection. And it's not an emotional "Yes!!" with double exclamation points. It's the unspoken, "God, please help me get this right." that comes from your soul. Your sincerity may be misdirected when you trust the wrong information. The guidance may be perfect for someone else but your happiness needs information that's perfect for you. It must embrace *your* purpose. You have to love it. When you see the love in your desires, the reason for your purpose pours out of you. Your love for anything is in your sincerity. It's your cosmic gyroscope. It's not important to be perfect. It's only important to want to be perfect.

If you try to do the right thing but miss, God will still help you because God loves your sincerity. You can always work on your accuracy. Your understanding has limits. Society feels safe with limits so there are times you'll be afraid to express yourself. Limiting yourself is uncomfortable but it helps you get by. Stylish clothes and jokes are often enough to satisfy society's sense of adventure. Too much honesty challenges it. Everyone you meet is a compromise. Your sincerity decides the limits you'll accept.

When your sincerity fits the accepted mold, you're welcomed whether you're a music fan or golf enthusiast. But, when you're different, your sincerity may cause a conflict. Your honesty is a gift to God and should be respected whether it reflects the community's view or something new you've discovered. While new paths should be questioned, reasonable ideas should be encouraged. Evolution always starts with a better idea.

So nurture your sincerity. It reveals who you are. It's the work of respecting yourself. Sincerity is super-satisfying in how its opposite can never be. Insincerity is a lie. But you don't just walk off a job because you don't like it. You have bills to pay. You can be sincere and still respect your unwelcome responsibilities. Surviving means sometimes you do things you don't like. So you accept an internal compromise until you can change things. Social manners can be a stretch. Still, nine times out of ten, it's the best way to get what you want. Others have to put up with you too. It's part of life's maintenance. You may not like it but it has to be done.

There's sacredness in sincerity that aligns your honesty with God's plan. It may be different from what your family told you. It might not be what society expects from you. But it'll be right for you and you'll love it. Personal leadership takes sincerity. When others are disappointed in you, your sincerity can accept their disappointment without accepting their opinion. You can accept their love without accepting their belief. Sensible people respect hard work and clear goals. You'll find your support come alive when the people who love you see you're not giving up.

God doesn't ask you to leave your comfort zone. God wants you to know your comfort zone. So it's important to create boundaries you trust. They shouldn't come from fear of someone's opinion, the fear that you're not who they think you should be instead of being who you are. Defenselessness is the absence of fear because there's no need for it. Defenselessness rejects fear. Defenselessness isn't surrender. It assesses a situation on the best thing to do and accepts the consequences as part of fixing the problem. It accepts what it can't change and moves forward. The miracle is that without fear, love can take its place. Do your best and don't worry about it. Through love you put your trust in God.

You can be honest but wrong. Your sincerity respects God through your honesty. Your sincerity seeks the truth even when you're mistaken. Right or wrong, it's important to trust your sincerity and accept that you can change your beliefs. If you make a mistake that hurts someone, all you can do is try to make it right. Love creates the balance in your heart to fix things. The sacred element in sincerity protects you even when you do something wrong. God will always support your desire to do what's right.

Life isn't easy. There can be hard choices to make between something bad and something worse. It may be laying off a good employee, sending a young person to prison, or leaving a secure life to risk your dreams. Life without choices doesn't challenge you. Your choices bring you closer to God. These are the times your intention is focused because the price of a mistake can be expensive. Your trust in love supports your sincerity. Ability only takes you so far. The rest of the way you go on faith.

Is nothing sacred? Can you be sincere and not love others? If you are sincere, isn't everything sacred? Isn't God everywhere in everything? There was a time professionals were respected for the important work they did for the community. Today, through endless media campaigns, a confusing healthcare system, and a complex justice system, their contribution is just another commodity with each one shouting "I'm the best." like they were all selling toothpaste.

Has today's culture, which is so interested in the emotional ping-pong of reality TV and gossip magazines, slid backwards on the convenience of social media and internet journalism so much that we don't give a damn about each other as long as it's entertaining? Ignorance makes mass communication a toy. Social values are trivialized instead of appreciating the struggles we all endure. You don't mature by ogling suffering or envying success. It's a mindless thrill watching misfits. There are no skills to appreciate. It's like kids playing tag. Reality shows are a valuable window on life when they reflect the hard choices of human relationships building a better world. But immaturity in compromising situations isn't a pretty sight if you love people.

Ask yourself, "Is watching people's problems a game or will you be a better person for it?" Will you embrace your emotions as guidance or drool over them like a mountain lion that's just taken down a deer? What do people mean to you? Do your values support your reality? Will you accept another person's moral weakness or will you stand up for the values you respect?

You know you're sincere when you're honest with yourself, and you know when your heart isn't in it too. Half-hearted attempts at cooperation disappoint everyone. When an adult forces themselves to ride a roller coaster to bond with their children, it only works when they have fun and repress their terror. Sincerity in love means showing the goodness in your compromises. If you're sincere, you don't want to communicate what you give up as a sacrifice, some debt with the expectation of payment. That's business, not love.

You control your sincerity because sincerity has two sides, what's in your heart and what you show in public. When you know your values, you can respect yourself no matter what the situation. You may not have the freedom to express yourself, but you always have the freedom of your feelings. Social relationships require that you compromise your sincerity in order to get along with others. It doesn't matter how you feel about them, you treat them with respect to promote cooperation. You might not like them, but they certainly like themselves. You accept a friend's wild ideas because your sincerity accommodates your love for them. You adapt your sincerity to the situation or you move on.

Everyone has responsibilities to others. It may be a friend who asks you for help on a day you're so busy you can't catch your breath or as trivial as someone trying to engage you in conversation about some self-serving complaint. Every day you make judgments about how much sincerity you're willing to share. Not everyone wants your sincerity. Some just want the companionship of your humanity and really aren't interested in you. You compromise your sincerity for the sake of the social benefits. Respecting your values in a social context is how life tests you. It may be as simple as smiling at someone you don't like. But it's important because everyone needs help.

Sincerity is your sanctuary. Not everyone can appreciate your dreams, but that's no reason not to have them. Your ambitions challenge you. Risk is an element of sincerity because it makes the potential in life real. People around you may be confronted because they're frightened by risk. To keep your social experience respectful, you have to respect your sincerity but you don't want anyone to be uncomfortable with it. Not everyone likes the opera or electronic video games. Look at the differences in music. Do you like rap, country, or rock? Respect creates the circumstances that let you express your sincerity and supports others in expressing theirs. It's the logic in manners. It helps you to work with people you don't know or don't like.

The highest value for sincerity is love. Sincerity is especially important when love comes to mating. Marriage and a family are lifelong commitments, usually with someone you barely know. Romance draws you together in its divine embrace. But it's hard to balance love's bliss with the clarity that matches your image to reality. You need validation for your feelings. You haven't lost all reason. How do you know the love is sincere? Is hearing "I love you." a thousand times enough? You'd like it to be and it helps but you need more proof. Love makes sense. Caring is the most dynamic emotion in life. Anger and hatred seem more intense, but they're self-consuming bursts, intense but temporary unless you hold onto them. Love connects you to the Universe. Love proves your sincerity.

Love is supportive, but *being in love* feels so good you may not want to leave an unsupportive relationship. Romance is the security in love, the trust. So trusting love allows you to release the intimate side of you, your erotic soul. The closer you get to your sexuality, the more you please yourself. Because it's so intimate, sex is very opinionated. So it has to be honest. It's a measure of your self-respect. There are good reasons; responsibilities to children, staying healthy, and respect for your partner. It's not the sexual act. It's how you feel about yourself and your partner. Love is the key to a romance that lasts. And your sincerity gives it to you.

Your sincerity believes in other people's sincerity, whether it's your lover or the corner grocer. You don't expect perfection. You expect honesty. How do you know if someone's being honest with you? Ask yourself, "What's best for you?" "What's best for them?" "What's a fair compromise?" Common sense is always fair. Then decide for yourself. Be alert to anyone trying to fool you into believing they're something they're not. It could be an innocent character trait or it could be a threat. Emotional hurts and lies often use a smile to hide the truth. A smile is approval and approval is safe. So ask yourself what's behind that smile when something doesn't make sense.

It takes time to be sure someone's sincere. If you can't be sure, at least be honest with yourself. First prove to yourself your own thoughts are sincere. You need a firm base to support your judgments. The picture of a person's values are their desires, sense of fairness, sense of responsibility, honesty, rationalizations, business ethics, religious beliefs, respect for others, and most of all their priorities. Then see what the person chooses and ask yourself if it fits the situation. If not, why not? You have to identify reasons sufficient to make a person do something you wouldn't expect. Your understanding of someone's sincerity is what you believe after your questioning is done.

Belief

Reality doesn't matter to your beliefs. What you believe is real to you. Your beliefs form a moral code that sets the limits of your compromises. If every moment you felt great, it wouldn't matter. But your daily mood challenges you to align your moral code with the changes in your life. Every day you have to face your values in a new round of challenging situations.

When you say "belief," you're describing your reality. It's not about the Loch Ness monster or an Elvis sighting. Those mysteries are questionable till proved. They're about how much proof you need to accept something that doesn't affect you. Conspiracy theories are different. Conspiracies are a real part of human nature. They have a history. They have a purpose. And they might affect you. A common occurrence is participants in a mystery getting older with the urge to set the record straight before they die. You still don't know if they're telling the truth or if they even know the truth but it adds believability to their argument since they don't have to face the consequences. Even if you immerse yourself in a mystery, it's still just a better educated guess. If it affects you though, "better safe than sorry" is a rational belief.

You need to believe in yourself. You've heard that a hundred times. It simply means that you accept responsibility for yourself. Failures, problems, deficiencies; none of that matters when you believe in yourself. Only your goal matters...and your intention to have it. You can only use what helps you. Discard the rest. You'd like things to be easy but life is what it is. Life is compared to a road, a path, or a journey because you move along it in steps. You mature through your experiences. All situations are temporary so don't despair and make things worse. You can only guarantee that your belief in yourself doesn't depend on your circumstances. Rough times are hard, but it's never your fault even when you make a mistake...unless you give up. You may not like the schedule, but you're winning as long as you believe in yourself.

Belief in yourself is learned. Some come to it more easily than others. That's human nature. Belief in yourself is being okay with who you are. The approval of those who love you supports you. The problem is, absent of those who love you, anyone's approval may be acceptable. But how can you believe what somebody tells you? First you have to ask yourself if they really care about you. It's easy to believe someone when they say nice things about you, especially if it's what you think of yourself. Their thoughts become an extension of your thoughts and those people become an extension of your well-being. You trust them, but you have to be careful because you're the one who'll pay if you're wrong.

Approval is important from the day you're born. You want to be sure you're doing things right. Approval is often mistaken for valuing you as a person instead of simply seeing right and wrong. Accepting who you are is self-approval. After everyone's opinion, the final approval is always yours. It's what you believe is your success. Approval confirms what you believe. Approval from people you respect matters. You can always use an extra set of eyes. You're taking a risk investing in yourself. You want to be right. You may not be right, but approval is as close as you can get.

What if the approval you get is wrong? From a loved one, it may be unconditional support not based on the facts. You evaluate friends, family, neighbors, and strangers on what you know about them; their experience and attitude. Then you assign a degree of belief to their approval. Life's a puzzle, like that game show where you guess the secret phrase by using the fewest number of letters. It's possible because the alphabet makes sense, language makes sense, and there's a history of phrases that makes sense. Life makes sense too and your common sense is a dependable way to make your decisions even when the details are missing.

Your purpose is more than your survival. Love is the minimum you're born with so you already have everything. You're already a winner. It may not seem like it, but your love survives your earthly sojourn while little else does. Everything about your life has value. Everything you do has a purpose. Lasting success doesn't mean amassing a great fortune you'll never spend. Life is about finding love in your daily efforts, including your regrets. Love isn't always joyful. Love connects you to God's experience in Creation. It's something you can believe in when your life seems unmanageable. Regardless of your problems, love is always reliable. It will always perform and it will always be there for you.

The human condition is meant to challenge you. It creates opportunities for you to evaluate your compromises and choose your priorities. It gives you internal conflicts to challenge your disappointments and external conflicts to challenge your fairness. Your job is to join them together in a philosophy where love is your priority despite your confusion. God won't leave you alone to suffer. God respects your burdens, including your thirst for success. Your backstop is God's attention. When you believe that, you'll find hope.

Belief in God takes different paths. There's the rote training you learn religiously where positive values are repeated until they become a fixed layer in your consciousness. You believe them because the people who love you tell you they're true. Since it makes sense and people use them successfully, you trust it. The problem is when you relinquish your will to the mechanics of rote teaching you can diminish the beauty in your creativity. To be a mindless follower may be socially acceptable, but belief in religious teaching is only a guide to your common sense. You're supposed to question it. Spiritual values prove their worth when you realize it's God's endless expressions of love that support you.

There's another way to believe in God. It's in your spirituality. It goes directly to the goal rote repetition is trying to teach. Then, through affirmations, you can use rote teaching to incorporate a practical understanding of what you already know. You'll never accept anything mechanical if it doesn't fit your beliefs. It's like a teacher taking a refresher course. You already know God. You just want to see where the boundaries are as you mature. How do your responsibilities change? What does God expect from you and what can you expect from God? It's the same right and wrong you're constantly testing. And it always ends in the same question, "What's love's role here?"

Your belief in God is a question. Your soul is your connection to God. Your humanity is God's creation but the rhythm you are as a human being exists in your questions. An answer is a brief condition intended to create more questions. Your creativity serves God's exploration of itself. Every trial, every victory, every failure is a wonder to God. God sees you grow in your challenges and loves you for it. Love empowers you beyond your trials. Conflicts provide the environment for love to test itself by creating more questions. Belief in God is belief in love. It's important to understand that your human condition is meant to align God's love with your soul's purpose and constantly test your values. This creates opportunities for you to create the joy you both want without worrying about a failure that will never be.

Believe in yourself as a soul. Your belief takes shape when you feel whole with God. You believe in yourself not as a supplicant but as an extension of God. Love can give you a feeling of failure when it's not appreciated. People have different levels of awareness and that makes the practical side of loving hard to trust. The relationship between love and life is a paradox of shifting values that creates opportunities. It's the challenge of being a boss or a parent. It's the good sense in, "Don't bite the hand that feeds you.", but still you get bitten sometimes. What never changes is how love resolves itself. And looking through God's eyes, there's plenty of time to get it right.

Belief in love isn't just about sex. Sex and romance are the obvious expressions of love. They combine love's spirituality with the human drive to mate. When they act together it's beautiful, but when they act selfishly souls suffer. Belief in love is your devotion to your respect for others. Romance is the test. It's blissful when successful but miserable when it fails. Spiritual love resolves that. It's unselfish. It looks for righteousness in relationships and doesn't feel any less if it's left out. It expects something better is coming. Without it, mental and emotional confusion can only offer disappointing human answers to what are really spiritual questions.

You know how love feels. The question is, "Is love an emotion like joy and hatred or more than an emotion?" You first meet love in your parents' hugs. Then you learn more from your siblings. You share it with your friends and learn the meaning of a "best friend." You experience "puppy love" and open a new dimension through sex. You share your love for your school and learn to love your culture and your country. You find a comforting variation of love in your prayers to God. You discover you can love a charismatic personality, like an evangelist or politician, as their words of wisdom touch your soul. Then you fall in love with a stranger and share the intimacy that touches every part of your life. You hug your kids and the cycle continues. It's not a leap to believe love is more than an emotion. It's a purpose. And it constantly seeks balance with your love for yourself.

Love is instinctive. It's part of every thought you have. So it's your choice to raise love from a sentimental concept to the way you live your life. That's the purpose of religion regardless of what you believe in. Your perspective is as valid as anyone's. Your access to love is only limited by your desire to know it. If you can't explain it like a theologian, you can still make enough sense of it to be happy. If you believe in love, you'll see it everywhere. Love is never hidden.

Love is why you believe in relationships. You expect a relationship to accept your love and love you back. That doesn't always happen. Loving someone or something doesn't mean you stop loving yourself. People are fallible and everything is temporal. That's why the concept of betrayal, having a selfish attitude towards love, is emotionally devastating. Spiritual love connects with emotional love and it's painful to separate them. It takes a mature person to respect love and give their emotions time to heal when they lose something they love. It takes experience to learn love can change and your trust in God still be whole. Having your happiness ripped away, seemingly rejected by God, is a shock. But recovering your belief, you know you can never be rejected by God.

Your belief that you're not alone is crucial. It's not easy understanding relationships. It takes work. It takes consideration. You may see finding your "soul mate" as a life-long accomplishment or merely a life raft sparing you from your miseries. You may disbelieve your hopes when you think a relationship is the only way life works. You get impatient. You grab whatever's handy and refuse to change even when you know it's not good for you. You refuse to understand things must run their course. Heartbreak, whether you learn it from a teenage break-up or from doing something that causes you to lose your self-respect, is one of the ways God proves itself. Loss doesn't destroy love. The question you should ask is, "What are you supposed to believe in when you think you're alone?"

Believe you're a loving person. All relationships start with you. But be reasonable. Not everyone's going to meet a beautiful model on the beach in Jamaica. You don't have to accept what the world is selling you. Trust your values. Love ends all differences. Arguments don't solve conflicts. Caring does. Love is the energy that moves in one direction, like a flock of birds. Positive relationships may seem disconnected, but love supports the individuals. Love is the one direction.

Belief in friends is comforting. Friendships are built on support. It doesn't mean you trust everyone. No matter how close they are, you know who you can rely on. Don't mistake a few laughs for dependability. It's easy to trust the wrong person because you know them well. Familiarity mimics trust when you should be watching their character. Consider who you're dealing with. Waiting for help may be inconvenient, but it's better than cleaning up someone else's mess. People act according to their nature. It's no guarantee you're right. It's just the best tool you have.

Believe in your intelligence. Trust your ability to make good decisions. Believe in yourself that you can answer any question if you have the time. Believe in routines, like the sun coming up each morning with the question, "Who'll win the race to the bathroom?" Repetitive motions are dependable so you know what to expect. It doesn't matter if you're a civil engineer planning a transit system for millions or trying to make sense of your health plan. Your belief in your intelligence tells you, *yes*, there's a sensible way things work.

Believe in your life as a member of society. You know you're alive but you're probably too busy to think about it. That's why you believe in government. You like a central authority protecting you and doing your thinking for you. You want to believe whoever's in charge cares about you. So you give responsibility for your life to someone you don't know and expect them to care about you like your mother. This is civilization. For all its complexities it works pretty well. That's why you believe in cooperation. That's the reason for government, organizing cooperation. You can curse its unfairness and inefficiencies. You can believe one system is better than another. But you can't deny you need it.

Believe in good health. Your health supports your confidence. It's *your responsibility* to protect it. Your body is predisposed to good health but life can stress you beyond your limits. You can't help getting sick. Accidents happen. But you can be conscious about it. Your health is an asset to Creation. Love connects you to strangers who'll readily come to your aid if they know you're not well. No reasonable person can find comfort as long as another is suffering. When you believe in yourself, good health becomes part of your character.

Believe in your purpose. Believe that you make it happen. You might believe it's to have more money or be more attractive. You might believe it's your family or service to humanity. You might believe it's to serve God. A suggestion may influence you but you choose to believe it. You know when your beliefs are satisfied or you'll doubt them till they are. They protect you so protect them. You insure them by demanding they be true. Deciding your beliefs takes work. Your beliefs may be mistaken, but your sincerity is enough to respect yourself. Beliefs matter because they support what's worth your commitment.

Feeling

You control *"feeling"* by embracing it. This isn't about joy, despair, or any of the feelings you know as emotions. This is about feeling as awareness, a supernatural sense, a woman's intuition, the moment you think, "This doesn't feel right." or "I don't know why but I've got to have it." It's hard to put reasons behind a feeling into words. Your intuitional logic works so fast you can't explain it. That feeling is your total awareness of the world. It's like when you're looking for a house. Suddenly you see one and without thinking you know it's right for you. The same goes for what repulses you. Feeling is important because sometimes your life needs speed. It's not the speed to go fast. It's the speed to instantly compare values. It doesn't have to be evaluated at the moment of decision. You just have to trust it.

Sometimes kindness feels right. You can feel your common sense, so to speak. You don't think about it, like when there's a disaster and you donate money for relief even though you don't know the people. But a request from a stranger is challenging. Your instinct is to help those in need, but you don't want to be tricked by someone playing on your feelings as you'd expect when you get a strange email from Europe asking you for money. And you're not going to interview someone holding a "Please Help Me." sign at a traffic light. To me, anyone who goes to the level of begging needs help. Even if your money goes to supporting their addiction, you're still helping them. You connect with human beings in your soul. We're all the same and when you reach past your fears you can feel it.

You can feel the mechanics of your life instinctively. Like the ebb and flow of the ocean's tides, you feel its balance. The whole planet maintains its balance in the same way you ride a bicycle. You guide the whole system in the direction you want. Energy expresses as an average, a compilation of everything affecting it. The difficulty is, because you're part of it, everything feels the same. Look for the unusual events that reveal the limits of the average and the patterns maintaining it. It's reverse engineering. You're looking for the interaction of the parts creating it. You can influence one part more easily than taking on the synergistic mass of its energy. It's easier to turn the wheel than picking up your bike and carrying it.

You evaluate your life by its ups and downs but its balance is where you are now. It's knowing what affects you that creates the balance. In the balance of history, things get done over time. God has a long term view. That's the conflict between God and human beings. It's the time it takes to solve a problem, the struggle. While human foibles are common so is the greater good of God's grace. You can feel the world's priorities shift because you're sensitive to its environment, its average. When you trust it, you'll feel it change before you know why.

When you acknowledge that *"feeling"* you'll make better choices. It's a skill that reacts quickly to make sense of things before you waste time analyzing them. It's more than training. It's the innate feeling that you always want the best for yourself. It's not a struggle of conscience. It's trusting your impression. Test it. Once you identify a feeling, compare your evaluations to where you might be if you hadn't trusted it. You may resist and add unnecessary criteria that muddle it up. You think how others might act, what if things go wrong, but mostly it's doubt in yourself. It's not easy when a paradoxical situation gives conflicting feedback and your choice is between two right answers. You have to accept yourself when you sacrifice something, like not stopping to help a stray dog when you're rushing to get home.

When you trust that *"feeling"* you can feel the love in others. You can feel the mood in others. Feeling is your subconscious awareness. In social situations, finding people you like matters. You want to know who cares about you and who cares about what they can get from you. Through feeling you qualify your relationships. You develop a feeling for friendships. When you feel something's not right, cordiality protects you if your heart's not in it. Not everyone likes you either. You're a human being trying to succeed and so is everyone else.

Feeling God is real. Your sense of God is always there but it's hard to see through the rigors of life. That's why religions take a day off for rest and reflection. It's easier to feel God when you limit your distractions. All spiritual techniques have the same goal, to separate you from your routines and give you a chance to ask yourself the meaning of what you're doing. Life isn't just about surviving. It's about questioning your purpose. It's not a passing thought or time to read a book. It's time to feel God in your soul.

How many times have you come to the end of your rope? You did your best then ran out of steam; no more energy, no more thoughts, no more feelings. Exhausted, you burned out. But you weren't done. You just needed rest to energize you for the next step. When you're rested, the individuality of things dissolves into a single entity and you can feel God. That's why religions emphasize the value of respecting everything. Issues with religion aren't about love. People object to rules that don't make sense to them. Religions provide a practical approach to God's love. There are many ways to look at the same thing. If you like the concept of religion, just pick one that feels right.

You can feel God physically, especially in your neck, back, and arms. It's a warm, comforting feeling. Unlike a drug, it's more delicate, more refined. You have to hold it tight to avoid any thought that might push it away. Honestly, I don't think you control it at all. It's more like a gift, a peaceful place where nothing can harm you. Even a moment of it is enough to prove God's existence. There's nothing else like it. It proves that somehow God makes sense. Feeling God is proof that you can trust love's support. You can savor it without limiting beliefs. You even feel a bit smarter. Just be aware of it. Sometimes it's an intuition, sometimes it takes years of study, but feeling God shows that you can trust God's love because you know it's real.

Attitude

Of all your conscious states, you have the most control over your attitude. Everyone has the same expectations. You can sympathize with them because social attitudes reflect common goals. The farmer on their tractor or the Wall Street banker on their computer have the same desire for love and success. But their attitude towards their environment determines their happiness. Attitude is a judgment.

Right or wrong, it's your trusted response. It's your protection. It underlies the facts and determines their value to you. It initiates your opinions. It colors your interpretations. It's your general outlook on the reasons for your beliefs.

Your attitude defines you. Your environment may make you a neighbor, a parent, an employee, or a boss. Each position puts you in a different circle of relationships. Though the relationships are different, you bring your attitude to all of them. Are you selfish or generous? You decide the attitude you think supports you. Changing your attitude is great if you can find a better one. Your attitude should be flexible. Sometimes cooperation works best and other times stubbornness works better. It shapes your decisions about who you are and how you see your relationships.

Your attitude can be safety in reticence, power in boldness, or superiority in self-righteousness. That's why your attitude is important in negotiations. You present the attitude you think is most effective. You express your feelings in your attitude. Disdain, adoration, competitiveness, persistence, reliability, those are attitudes too. Attitudes can be positive, "Somehow things will work out." or negative, "Something's got to go wrong." It's the story of the optimist and the pessimist. Is the glass half-full or half-empty? It's a human trait that can be found in Sumerian writings 5,000 years old. It's frustrating though when your heart says "yes" but your attitude says "no." And it doesn't have to be your own to affect you.

What do you do when a bad attitude overrides your common sense? The danger is a bad attitude can become a bad habit, a substitute for your personal responsibility. If your attitude shares a group belief, then you'll go wherever the group goes. You'll share its rewards and bigotries. But there's no guarantee that attitude is right. Religious and political attitudes can be divisive and strange when their claimed purpose is love and respect. Many traditional attitudes are immaturities unable to cope with their evolving culture. Though you share a group's attitude, it's only an influence. You're not bound to it. Your attitude is yours alone. The attitude you choose may be born from a group, but it's accepted *by you*.

191

While your physical senses form your first impression, your attitude forms your next impression. Before you know someone, you have a feeling about them. You have an idea of what they're doing and why. Your second impression, your attitude, guides and evaluates your questions about them. Based on those values, you judge them. The competitive nature of survival makes your attitude crucial in managing your relationships. Is your attitude, "Live and let live." or "Get with the program." You accommodate human nature because you understand people have moods. That's why it's important to have a positive attitude. Your attitude matures as you gain an appreciation for life's difficulties. You become more generous and sympathetic. Life teaches you that often the bridge between hope and desperation is a simple change in attitude.

Your attitude towards God matters. Whether you see yourself as part of God's plan or alone taking your turn in a godless Universe, you have an attitude towards your existence. Whether your attitude is self-serving or selflessly considerate is an attitude you choose. People with religious beliefs have a reverent attitude toward how their faith affects their relationships. You have an attitude that serves your own idea of fairness. You're a creative human being. You have free will. Having an attitude about your consciousness is unavoidable. You might as well be conscious about it. Then you're not just being creative. Then you're being wise.

Your attitude determines your relationship to God. You do your best to trust God's love or you decide there's no use for it. You just want to make your life better. Trusting God's love doesn't mean you won't have problems. It's meant to help you decide the values that give your life meaning. Faith, hope, and charity are your purpose realized through God's plan for you. Life's ups and downs concern you, but an attitude that trusts God is just common sense.

Knowing: Trusting Your God Sense

You have a magical nature, a wisdom mysterious in how it's a bit more sensitive than what you think you know. It's reasonable and loving. It's your connection to God. It's the symmetry of existence in a mystical dance beyond life and the accomplishments you prize so much. It's the ideal you revere in love. It's your purpose beyond your survival. It's hard to touch. You're used to the friction of your responsibilities, so you adore the comfort you find in love. You begin to rely on it. That's your purpose; fulfilling God's imagination through love. It's a reasonable challenge but hard as hell sometimes. It's your soul testing love's values against its unlimited freedom.

Knowing, like *"feeling"*, can be hard to come to terms with. It challenges your normal beliefs. It asks you to trust your spiritual sense. It's so intimate it can be frightening. And it can make you feel superior when you know someone's belief is wrong. You're not alone. More or less, *knowing* is happening to everyone. There's another level of consciousness between your body and soul. Spiritual values have to be communicated somehow. Religions come from somewhere. Giving people insight into the grand scheme is a good way to get them to think about their values. All of a sudden, something makes sense and you know it comes from God. It's important to know you're worthy, because you definitely know it's happening.

Knowing is God's gift of knowledge for you. It's God's love, respect, and confidence in you. When you realize it's happening, even when it's hard to hold onto, it's beautiful. It's like seeing a rainbow. You enjoy it, then it's gone and there's nothing you can do to make it stay. But you expect it'll happen again sometime. Even though it lasts only seconds, you trust it more each time.

Respect your moments of "*knowing*" even if you don't think you're that smart. It's not wisdom from experience. *Knowing* is the wisdom that comes from God. It's your spiritual common sense. This is the "from the mouths of babes" wisdom. It's divine, loving, and real. There's no wrong way to do it. You're meant to have it and you don't need thirty years of spiritual disciplines to justify it. You just have to want it. It comes when God feels it's right. You can't avoid God and you can't "un-know" things. If your beliefs conflict with your *knowing, and you reject your knowing*, the truth doesn't change. If God wants you to get a message, you'll get it, and you'll keep getting it until you accept it. God trusts that one day you'll know the right answer.

Being and Your Personal Philosophy

"Being" is the philosophy behind your choices. You walk a line between your human and spiritual selves. You choose your values from both sides. It's the reason for your life in a world that doesn't seem to have any reason. Everything is temporary. It's rare that you'll do anything remembered by history. Most historical figures are curiosities, their achievements easily forgotten in the modern race for fame.

"Being" is your personal directive. You're a human being one way or another. When you make your *sense of yourself* a priority you can improve it. Your spirituality works through your humanity. You control it through your choices. It's as close as you can get to being a wild animal. Your goal is to tame the beast to be your friend. Who doesn't thrill at seeing a horseback rider galloping through the brush? Your life is waiting for you to ride it...and willing to help you. So trust yourself and let yourself go.

"Being" is your personality, so love it. Know who you are and who you want to be. Question yourself. Accept what life gives you. Improve it. Fix your mistakes without recrimination. Don't be afraid of who you are. When you love yourself, you live your spirituality. Release your fears. Remember when you first learned to swim and came to when you had to let go of the pool and swim on your own. Today it might be public speaking or opening a business. Your support is there but you still have to let go. You have to do it. Now swimming is fun. Fear is only useful until you find a better way. Experience teaches you confidence so don't run from it. Common sense tells you when you're ready. Trust yourself and you'll be yourself. And you'll like yourself.

Sex: Your Second Soul

Your consciousness isn't complete without sex. It's a consuming state of being that mere mating doesn't explain. You're always open to sexual attraction whether you're married or single. It's no wonder societies have rules about it. Sex's powerful attraction creates moral responsibilities. Your self-control is challenged because there's wildness in your humanity. That's why social attitudes towards sex

194

matter. Most societies agree there are more benefits in a committed union than to engage sexually with countless partners and ignore the cost in health and trust. There's a gulf between what's publicly respected as the right attitude towards sex and the lack of self-control people find difficult to resist when they're sexually excited. That's why there are laws about sexual relations. Disrespectful sex creates victims.

You accept your sexual nature so you can live in peace with others' sexual natures. Sex needs agreement. It's a negotiation. It can be as simple as a flirting wink or as complicated as a second marriage with a half dozen kids and multiple sets of in-laws. So there's a need for rules that respect everyone's sexuality. The only rule you can trust is love. It's love for sex and the right of every human being to satisfy themselves. It's not easy when governments, religions, and social trends infuse themselves into what should be a simple agreement between adults. Cultural extremes and criminal behavior add to the confusion. It leads to wantonness and inhibitions. "I don't care." and "I don't want to care." And you have to make sense of it all to have a happy sex life.

You have a sexual body, an erotic soul like your physical, mental, and emotional bodies. When you get horny, or whatever you call it, your sexual arousal engrosses your being. You want to embrace it without crossing the line. So you wink at prostitution, pornography, dirty jokes, affairs, and all the sexual innuendos in the media because you like being sexual. The problem is how strong it can be and how inconsiderately it can express itself. You don't want to intrude on anyone but you want very much to find partners to share your sexuality. That's why testing it is a game. The one rule of responsibility is love. Love means respecting other people's beliefs. When it comes to sex, people are all over the place. Some are open and others repressed. Sexual attitudes evolve and then repeat themselves. There are only so many things you can do. Prudish or libertine, your sexual peace is in your honesty and respect for others. And it grows just like your other bodies.

Attraction comes before reason. You're sexually attracted to a stranger. They may be good-looking or plain but something about them excites you. You don't know their background or anything about them important to a mutually supportive relationship. All you want is to be with them. Sex is personal. You control your opportunities. You can spend all night at a bar, join a dating service, or belong to an organization with a social aspect. You can pick the right time to go to the market when you think there's a chance you might meet someone. You can ask for an introduction or approach a stranger with a "line" about something you have in common. You want to know if there's an equal interest. Here's a caveat. Ask yourself if you're really feeling your sexuality or just trying to prove your self-worth.

Follow the tabloids if you want to see how trivialized sex can be. It might be called *Lifestyles* but it's about sex. Body image, affairs, dating, divorce, sexual orientation, over and over the media sells you strangers' lives in their quest for your attention. If you missed it, it wouldn't affect you at all. Sex is interesting because it excites you. It's your nature. Think about your family. Sex connects every part of it. It created generations of your relatives. And it all starts with how you deal with your sexual relations.

You constantly transmit sexual energy. You control it. You can dress to accentuate it when you're on a date or tone it down at work. You know the type of partner that excites you. You know the iconic expressions of sex appeal like Marilyn Monroe and Elvis Presley. They're so attractive it goes beyond any type. But you expect more from a mate than sex. Survival takes work. You can't deny your sexuality, but you need more for a successful relationship. You need support.

You have the urge to mate. You have that impulse whether you like it or not. Attraction is as natural as the beauty God gave the peacock. You use a fit body, fashionable clothes, a cool haircut, an impressive car, financial success, intelligence, humor, courage, cosmetic surgery, and even lie about your age to be more attractive. Dancing, the ritualistic rhythm of your body's sensuality, is beautifully sexual. From seductive, animalistic gyrations to the gentle romance in a slow dance, your sexuality expresses itself positively through dancing.

196

Romance mixes sex, looks, interests, attitudes, family, goals, and trust...but not in equal parts. You decide the compromises you'll accept. Then you look for someone to care about and fall in love. It's fun, but infatuation can easily overcome your common sense. Being in love is so comforting you might do anything to keep it. Or you might see love as ownership instead of loving someone even when you're out of the picture. It all comes with maturity. But you may not be that mature, especially when you can't count on easy sex anymore. You like what you had. It's hard to find and difficult to give up. That's why you get married. You want an agreement you can count on, especially for your kids. With so much at stake, you need love's support.

Your soul is connected to all other souls. In the same way every cell of your body supports you; this combined conscious existence supports God. God generates love. Love is sexual too. Love helps you understand sex's contradictions. God's beauty is the union of contradictions with every relationship an opportunity to create more love. Sex connects you to God through the miracle of mating. So your sexuality is holy but it often conflicts with your human passions. Marriage means you reserve yourself for one partner to strengthen your commitment and create more love through a family.

Rules about sex serve society. It's important because sex creates relationships. Sexual intimacy binds you to a partner. Even a one night stand connects you forever. Relationships rely on trust. Fidelity doesn't mean you're just sexually trustworthy. That trust supports your whole partnership. Fidelity is about dependability. A broken bond threatens your faith in everything. You want to be your sexual self but there's a wider range of support that matters to a relationship. It's important to be honest. Talking about sex is a mix of inhibitions seeking common ground. The more you respect yourself, the more fun talking about sex is. The more humble you are, the more exciting talking about sex is. Your sexual explorations often end with the person you marry. What makes sex fun is knowing everyone's a bit confused about it. Talking honestly about anything helps you mature. You may have to work through generations of judgments to find your comfort zone, but eventually you do.

Sex requires responsibility because it needs permission. It's more than just a thought or feeling. You share your sex physically. Besides making money, it's the most judged pursuit in society. Your sexuality is constantly on. It's up to you to be respectful about it. Sexual mores are revised to keep pace with evolving social standards. It still has to be positive for you to respect yourself. The media exposes everything you could imagine about sex. Add to it everyone's opinion, religious traditions, and government regulations. Then you have to sort through it all to find a compromise that satisfies you. Being sexually responsible challenges your body. You want to satisfy your urge for sex and enjoy the pleasure that makes sex fun. Love is still the supreme element in any judgment. Balance your sex drive with love and you'll free your erotic soul.

Chapter 9
Controlling Eternity

Furthermore

Writing is easy for me. The ideas keep popping in my head. Maybe it's from a past experience or it could be that angel whispering in my ear. Maybe it's a memory from a dozen lifetimes ago. It's the miracle of my awareness. It's my consciousness. There's value I want to share so I write it down to express my ideas in a way that's comfortable for the reader. It's like a sculptor chiseling a block of stone into the image they see in their mind, chipping and polishing layer by layer. First I put my ideas on paper. That's the easy part. The time-consuming part is eliminating the clutter. It's getting the cadence right so the content stays in tune with the reader. It has to flow from word to word and paragraph to paragraph. It's creating a clear picture because I want the reader to trust it. It's not that hard. It just takes time.

The beauty of multiple drafts is the progression. It's the process of peeling away the layers to get to the core ideas. Going over the same ground is vital to simplifying the message. When a paragraph doesn't read right it usually means something needs to be cut or a transition is missing, some sentence or phrase that clarifies the connection between ideas. Every draft is done on a different day so I'm in a different mood. It applies different parts of my personality to the same question. I can describe it from different points of view. All the while I'm growing as a person. Many times I've had something happen to me and used it in the book the next day. Multiple looks gave me time for the book to mature.

That's the work of writing. That's the work of life. It's an inspiring quote that 99% of writing is perspiration and 1% inspiration. But perspiration and inspiration isn't just for writers. It's in everything you do. And it isn't chiseled in stone. You can create more inspiration. Your desire to know God creates the psychological environment that invites God into your life. Then you're not depending on your hard work with the passing chance you'll catch a low-flying blessing. It won't be 99% your responsibility. You can make it fifty-fifty. You can create an equal partnership with God. Just ask.

What did you expect?

Is this how you thought it would be? It's not like the ads on TV but you can get pretty close. That's what you share with the advertisers. You have a vision of happiness. It becomes the plan for your life. You see what you want and go for it. You can start anywhere at any time. You do things that help you and avoid the things that hold you back. Those advertisers' dreams are something to aspire to. You know about war and falling in love. You've been through good times and bad. Old friends die and you grieve, then you meet a new friend and share a good laugh. The vicissitudes of life, but why all the pain? Why can't it all be good times? You've seen the old movies. Other than the fashions, nothing changes. Human nature is the same. You mature, of course. Everyone changes like that. Then what's the value of anything? Is success an achievement or just a direction?

If you decide eternity is real then you should have a plan for it. That's the purpose of religion. It's a model of behavior to help you make choices about your future. Religion's main theme is love, expressed through honesty and trust, can expect justice. Even without eternity, religion is good guidance for a dependable society. The world will continue after you're gone. You may consider a cataclysm might destroy the world but I don't think you'll deny the Universe will go on. That's why you make plans for your remains and how you want your possessions distributed after you die. With everything gone the question remains, "Does your sense of yourself disappear or do you somehow continue?"

What happens when you die?

Do you have eternal responsibility? If you followed the "rules" have you won the game? Will you receive your rewards in eternity? But, an eternity to do what? That's a long time to keep busy. After all the sacrifice you invested in life, it doesn't make sense your experience should end there. Is it all wasted if you weren't successful? Your thoughts, feelings, and actions are your life, so where's the value in doing them right if you disappear when it's over? If you lived according to God's laws will your eternity be happy but if you lived selfishly eternity will punish you forever? Who in their right mind would gamble that? It doesn't make sense to risk forever on eighty years of abandoned responsibility; much of it spent learning to be a mature person who can even make a responsible decision. Life is reasonable. An aspect of religion is to show how your priorities affect you. Eternity sees your values. Eternity respects life's pressures. Eternity's judgments are loving. It *is* how you play the game. There's no winning or losing. Winning is baked in the cake.

All religions have ideas on what happens to you when you die. Who knows? People don't come back and talk about it. There are mediums who claim to talk to the dead. There's the belief in ghosts. There are stories about people at the brink of death leaving their body, seeing a tunnel, speaking to angels, and then reawakening. I believe when it's said Jesus saved the world, accenting love is what they mean. He came to help the human race. So why was his death unique? Because he survived beyond his death. And why has Jesus' last question puzzled theologians, "Dear God, why have you forsaken me?" I think the question was a parting gift from God for a job well done. What kind of gift do you give the Lord of the Universe? A question he couldn't answer.

Born Again: The Cycle of Reincarnation

Everything runs in cycles. You know when to get up and what you'll do that day. You understand the cycles of a day, a month, and a year.

You rely on cycles repeating themselves. You rely on knowing things will happen a certain way at a certain time. Then you can prepare for it. You may not be able to change a cycle but you can work with it. The machines you use run in cycles. The electricity that powers those machines runs in cycles. Windmills and waterwheels run in cycles. Cycles control energy. The tides ebb and flow. The seasons change with the Earth's orbit around the Sun. Everything about your life runs in cycles. So if this is so obvious, why shouldn't your soul recycle too? You're born, mature, then pass on. The question is, "Is this the end of your existence or just another cycle?"

That's what the reincarnation question asks. Is there a cycle where your conscious self is reborn? Multiple lives create a depth of understanding that proves love can be successful in any situation. It's God's way of being sure you've seen everything. From incurable diseases to breaking some record, you explore life's limits. You compete with others and compete with yourself. You may laugh about a bad experience later but it's usually not a belly laugh. There's a poignant way you laugh that respects the paradox between joy and suffering. An experience may be severe but relative to eternity your soul embraces any challenge. A lifetime is a drop in the bucket. It doesn't feel like it when it's happening. It may be beyond your endurance, but it's not beyond your soul to try again. I imagine souls getting together after their lives joking about the time they had here, sharing their joys and sorrows like old friends around the kitchen table. God keeps the process obscure so you'll keep coming back.

The Evidence in Ethics

What's the purpose of recycling spiritual energy? Besides exploring the different aspects of being human, I think reincarnation maintains the spiritual cohesiveness of the Universe in the same way atomic particles hold their structures together through their recycling orbits. There's an orderly movement of souls in and out of spirit. It's a guess based on the ethical nature of love. Love cares about everything. Recycling allows more souls to enter the system just like getting back in line for another ride on the roller coaster. With all the souls working together, God's love grows. Ethics help you maintain love's values in the confusing excitement of this self-charging energy.

You want to be ethical. Ethics are the standards you live by. Your standards evaluate your responsibilities and the rule of love in your relationships. Love doesn't compromise. It's always complete. Look for the balance between you and anyone you meet to determine what they want and how it affects you. Look for the material compromises. You don't live in a vacuum. You're part of a system that requires your involvement. You can choose any lifestyle you want but you can't avoid social order. Ethics are your responsibility to be respectful. You may play a role in life but you can't fake your ethics. You can't fake love. The question is, "Are you being ethical?"

You take society's rules and match them to your values to create your ethics. Ethics are your values in considering others. You create a measure of fairness and respect. The evidence of ethics is that there's a negative side to not being ethical. You suffer emotionally when you do something unethical because you know it's wrong. You know it's selfish. It conflicts with the eternal truth that every soul is created in love and for all our differences one love is who we are. It's your soul's mandate to cooperate. Cooperation reflects love. Everyone shows up at work at the same time because you depend on your coworkers so you can do your job. You work together because you all want to pay your bills.

"Do you think you're a good thief?" Most people would be disgusted at the thought they'd even be considered a thief. Most people prize honesty and would never steal anything from anyone. But there are people who steal without compunction, proud of themselves, and make a career of it. They go against the social order and if they're caught they can go to jail. The odd thing is even thieves are thought to have ethics. There's the "honor among thieves" myth that you don't inform on your fellow criminals. It's an anti-social attitude with an ethical twist. The conundrum is if you only get one chance at life why would ethical thoughts exist? Why would it matter if you were a thief or a murderer as long as you didn't get caught? Yet people do feel regret. Remorse is God's love challenging your selfishness. There'd be no reason to care if you didn't have a sense of future responsibilities. The fact that you're concerned, even when no one else knows, is proof that ethics exist and eternity is real. You might argue it's ingrained training, but how do you feel when you've been slighted? Do you feel it instinctively or is it something you learned?

Knowing Who You Are

If you want a voice in eternity you have to know who you are. It's the thoughts behind your actions that identify you, your reasons. When you die, all you take with you is your consciousness. If the concept of reincarnation is true then you've been working on it a long time. You really don't know why things happen. God's the judge. It's your motives that matter to you. You're your own loving mentor. You have a moral sense of what you believe is right and wrong. Morals aren't specific as much as you're doing your best with what you have. The value in a moral outlook is knowing that though God's gifts aren't shared equally, God's love makes everyone equal.

It reasons that your goals end with your passing even though your consciousness and the love you created continue. That's the purpose of life. Spirit isn't governed by a new set of rules once you die. In spirit the rules crystallize so you can express yourself without life's limits obscuring your efforts. There's a cleansing nature to eternity where love bathes you in kindness and forgiveness. You become clear on how to improve your character to align more with love. I don't know what's around the next corner but I'm sure love is part of it. Your life is lived and forgotten, but your love goes on forever. Love is everything. That's why creating love is important while you're alive. You have opportunities in life's resistance that aren't available in the ethereal realm of spirit. All the qualities of character you aspire to, you learn through love. Love is your goal. You just have to know where you're coming from.

You create the person you are.

Who do you want to be? Free will is a great concept but it's not easy being human. You don't start off knowing how to use your free will. You have to learn how to use it responsibly. You have to learn about relationships and priorities. You have to learn to use your creativity respectfully. You have to appreciate how things react. Then your experiences help you mature. You know what you like and don't like, the things you have a talent for and those that are a complete mystery no matter how many times they're explained. But you were never a blank slate. You had inclinations. The infant you were in your crib already knew where you were going.

Your nature, religious training, community ideals, and parental guidance start you on your way. You choose your goals and work toward them the best you can. You create your life with a purpose in your soul from before you were born. You don't arbitrarily meet life. Everything about you looks for what resonates with you. So what attracts you? Your maturity shows you. Maturity releases your inhibitions to reacquaint you with yourself. You're an evolving person. You may do something because someone tells you it's right, but your happiness comes from you. Survival is a distraction but it keeps you alive. The problem is when your survival surpasses your purpose and you put more trust in material values than you do in love.

Who you are fits the model you form in your psyche. You are who you think you are. You manage your ideas with that goal in mind. You have the pieces. You have the vision. All you need is the right attitude. Success or failure is an attitude. You believe you'll succeed or you think you'll fail. Or you ignore it altogether because you don't think it's worth your time. Your attitude guides your imagination. Your imagination is a sensing device, like radar. It searches the horizon for your beliefs reflected in life's possibilities. Your soul directs you to your peace. The person you create wants the comfort in your peace. You can trust your security to God or trust it to an image of materialism that lets you rationalize it. You can drive a car you like or drive a car others think is right for you.

Do you have a plan for eternity?

You should. If you benefit from living an ethical life it should serve you in your next life too. But serve you how? It's not as simple as heaven, hell, or nothingness. After your recent sojourn you still have choices to make. You have your latest life to review but now with clear standards to judge it by. There's the old right and wrong again or, at least, loving or not loving. You still need to know where you are and where you want to be. In a way you're back where you started. It's like getting ready each morning for a new day. You shower, comb your hair, and start out hoping for the best. But nothing really changed. You're just free for a moment from your trials. So it's easier to get in touch with your values again. Eternity's purpose is its endless opportunities. All you need is to juggle two things: you and love.

Through each life you explore Creation. You might ask, "If you're perfect in God's love, what else is there to do?" That's the problem with perfection. What do you do with your creativity? You see a finished puzzle. Once it's complete you mix it up and start again. But each time you do it a little differently. One time you start in the middle, the next time you start at the edge. God is a mystery to itself. God asks the same questions you ask. God answers those questions through you. It's no accident that you're creative. You're designed so you can explore these questions. Like God, there's no answer for your awareness, only the love that blesses your existence. That's the problem with puzzles. The answer doesn't answer anything. You may not be an inventor who can imagine something and build it out of parts in your garage, but you can always think of something that makes your life better. Often it's building better relationships. That's your plan for eternity. It's to create more love by giving and receiving love. The uncertainty of your survival makes it a puzzle. The answer isn't in solving anything. The answer is in asking.

Self-evaluation *After* You Die

As in life, you have to figure out what you'll do in your afterlife. You create love because you have an eternal sense of yourself. Many religions teach that you live your life for your responsibilities to your afterlife. I don't know what each religion's rules are. I don't know what priorities you'll have. I'm not sure what resources you'll have. I see who I am and how people value their priorities. I see the changes in individuality and the continuity in life. I see human beings with a predictable nature. I see the physical world and its nature. I see consciousness, logic, and imagination. I see choices. I believe in divine intervention and messages from spirit whose intention is to help you understand the mystery. I believe there's a purpose in everything. I believe you have a purpose. If this is all true, then when you leave this earthly plane you'll have to evaluate how well you did and what improvements you can make to be a better soul. With whatever new awareness comes to you, you'll make your judgments. It just makes sense.

Now your soul has decisions to make from a spiritual point of view. Every life was a test. Now your soul has to decide how well you did and how you matured. Matured into what, God knows. It's a safe bet it's about love. You've heard about karma, how you're responsible for your past crimes and kindnesses. I don't know how reincarnation's debts work but I know love solves everything. It may not have a linear solution that takes you from an obvious point A directly to point B. The result of what you do today may have many twists and turns before it resolves itself, and millennia to do it. That's your challenge. You have to be sincere and trust God's plan. If love doesn't satisfy you, something's wrong. You have one asset that evaluates everything correctly. Love. Everything else is a reflection that can be easily distorted.

Can you design your life with eternity in mind?

What's your plan for eternity? It's not an unknown. You use your life to create it. Your soul knows God and your consciousness knows life. They're inseparable and depend on each other. Imagine yourself in Spirit. How would you design your life? You know the experience life offers. You know its problems too. But here's where your consciousness and soul diverge. Your soul doesn't want to avoid your problems. Your soul uses them. It's easy for your soul to be enthusiastic about tackling things you want to avoid. Illness, poverty, confusion, failure, war, crime, accidents, disasters, "Oh!" your soul muses, "What an opportunity to rise above it all and praise God's glory." Your soul doesn't feel alone. Your soul is an individualized expression of God's purpose. Your soul knows one day you'll finish your life and everything will pass. For your soul, there are only benefits, only choices reviewed in God's loving light. Can you design your life with eternity in mind? That was always God's plan.

Religion: A Beginning

You might think it's beyond you, you're okay without it, no one talks about it, so how could it be important? But eternity, you don't want to make a mistake that lasts forever. Whatever your approach, you have no control other than your desire to do well. As a human being, you're a synergistic creation of God's living purpose. God is there, your soul is there, your personality and human desires are there, but now you have reality's competitive nature testing how you use love to achieve your goals. The question is, "If you accept love is eternal, how does it affect your choices today?"

I love religions but where did they come from? It's easy to list the seers who accepted God's inspiration to explain our existence and share it with others. God created miracles to prove there was something special about what they had to say. But you can say anything and attribute it to God. Saying something's a message from God awes people. People want to know what God has to say and how they can live a righteous life. That's the controlling aspect of religion. Some like it, others don't. God created religions to help explain your responsibilities. God made a lot of them so you'd find one you like. There are no superior religions. Love is the essence of all religions. Religions provide the basic rules that help you decide your values. In that way even atheism is a religion. While your commitment to a doctrine may give you peace of mind, only love will satisfy your soul...only love.

Success or Failure: The Value in Problems

Success and failure don't exist in eternity. Only love exists reflected in your questions. Eternity is your chance to learn as much as you can about love. The difficulty with life is you can't always count on intense situations to enlighten you. Much of life is monotonous. Eternity solves that problem. Eternity is a timeless oneness complete in itself like some perfect machine creating more and more love. Like Einstein's famous explanation of the feeling of time speeding up as the hours pass quickly when you're spending time with your lover, "Is it over already?" But eternity never ends. Love defines eternity's timelessness, so it's a good way to look at it.

Life's stuff doesn't affect eternity. Love does. It's God's weird joke. Spiritual logic is the reverse of conscious logic. In spirit you're not measured by who built the tallest building. You're measured by the love you shared. You're constantly confronted by questions that test your love. When a person fails, they're reviled as weak. That may be true, but it's not how they're judged in eternity. Regardless of your shortcomings, eternal success is measured by the love you create. Life is short. Eternity is endless. Your soul isn't going anywhere. It means you should live the best life you can that respects your spiritual values, the values you take with you when you die.

You grow. That's why you're alive. You want the opportunities love gives you. Success is in your maturity. Maturity is love growing in you. You explore love through life's limits. Your maturity finds a balance then asks, "Where is love here?" It's like Rudyard Kipling's poem "If." Failure isn't an obstacle and success isn't a goal. They're challenges. The question becomes, "Now that you're free from the pressures of your accomplishments, how can you use your maturity?" If you see success and failure as conditions to explore, then you're on your way. That you can put in your eternal bank account because maturity is love; love for yourself, love for others, and love for God.

How will you be remembered? How will God remember you?

Spiritual success isn't in your accomplishments. Spiritual success is in engaging your life with a loving attitude. Humanity prizes a supportive mate and a good income to make your life comfortable. After that, life gets tricky. Your creative nature doesn't stop once you have your comforts. You still want things, whether it's ending world hunger or baking a great pie. As you mature, life becomes more manageable. Your relationships flower. You gain experience. It's comforting. So what could ruin this? Nothing. You just need the right attitude.

People make an impression. It could be an incident or their everyday behavior. You identify who you like and who you don't. You won't remember everyone. Even fame passes. The thing about fame is you can be an awful person, do one good thing, and that's how history remembers you. The reverse is true too. There are wonderful human beings who by some twist of fate are remembered as bad people. Still, accurate characterizations are most likely. It takes a historian to make a fair judgment. No one is all good or all bad. There's love in everyone. God knows your trials. Even when fate pushes you in the wrong direction, God still loves you.

It's like interviewing for a great job...and getting it! It's your accomplishment over uncertainty. God knows your potential. Eternity asks you to look to the future. Your soul's guidance is your *conscience*. You might ask, "If your soul knows so much, how come you're not happy?" Dissatisfaction directs you to what you do want. There's a right and a wrong way to do things. What's right is loving and hopeful. What's wrong clings to material solutions as if you could take them with you when you die. There's logic in eternity. After you die, what's worth having? The image stays here. Love and your character are eternal. Your character is your awareness of love's priorities. Your connection to love is eternal. That's what you increase. There's no penalty for not doing it. Whatever you accomplish, you'll always have an equal measure of God's gratitude.

The Value in Values

Your values show up in your choices. It's what you believe is worth what you want. Love empowers you. You can feel it wholeheartedly or block it as a weakness. You're probably confused about the best way to use it. Your life reacts to threats, even as simple as someone cutting you off on the highway. In your thoughts you breed the resentments and rationalizations you use to protect yourself. The trick to defeating selfish thoughts is defenselessness, releasing your fears so love can replace them. Offense is how you accomplish your goals. Love is about winning, not avoiding losing.

Human values and spiritual values aren't so different. They both define your relationships. You're an individual in body and soul. You have free will to question everything and accept the answers that make sense to you. You have a responsibility to God's wholeness, something easily confused when your survival depends on everyone looking out for themselves. So how do you fit in this chaotic mélange? How do you harmonize with God's plan of conflicting right answers? It seems it would take forever to figure out and that's exactly what it takes. It takes eternity.

What is mass consciousness in eternity?

Eternity is so obscure how could you possibly think you affect it? Religions do their best to explain how your choices have meaning. They believe your daily thoughts define the values you trust in eternity. Like anyone seeking comfort, you join with others for support. You share the benefits of everyone's experience. You grow socially as a soul. In eternity, conflicts are opportunities to create more love. Love's perfection blesses every compromise that treats you fairly.

You can reject mass consciousness's negative aspect when it ignores your individuality. But if you respect your individuality within it, you can reap its benefits. It's the glory God imbued in our collective consciousness. Mass consciousness asks, "How can we all do better?" But it's confronting. People have different views from different points of view. I'm sure you have an opinion on how the government spends your taxes. Love respects honest views on common interests. Talk about politics is good even when you disagree. Talk about social responsibility is good because it makes demands on everyone. Mass consciousness is where your beliefs average out with others in the community. It's important because social rules respect the average.

Mass consciousness reflects the consciousness of the group you belong to. It could be a political affiliation or other sports fans who love the same team you do. All souls unify in love. Love is God's all-inclusive consciousness. You try to duplicate love's perfection, but on Earth it's easier to bond in a logical theme because everyone has their own idea of what makes sense. Things make sense depending on what you want; sunshine for a day at the beach or rain so you can curl up with a good book. Even when its purpose dangles from a single, personal thread, you like the safety in agreeing with others. That's why voters choose their leaders by race or gender instead of judging them by their history. Mass consciousness supports you. And if you have any doubts, eternity will always find a new niche for you.

Eternity helps everyone solve the same problems but from different points of view.

It's the same for everyone. Human nature drives your survival and spiritual nature steers your existence. Your instincts keep you pointed towards your goals. You understand spiritual things innately, but you have to learn how to relate them to life. You have values to assign and ideas to trust. While the essential problems are the same, your resources are different. People are born with different opportunities. You play the game the best you can with what you have. As you grow, you sharpen your skills. Then you find a balance where you can be a loving person without compromising yourself. You constantly refine your character knowing you're maturing.

It's doable but you need support. Eternity is your support. You don't accomplish everything in a lifetime. There's much too much and it's unbelievably complex. Your personality needs reinforcement to trust the flux. So you live by habits. Habits are your comfort, your reasonable expectations. Like training for a sport, you want to increase your abilities. But it takes time. Your plan to change your character is the most difficult thing you'll do. It's your willingness to confront your habits when you're not even sure what they are. It's your willingness to confront the positive and negative aspects of your character when you're not sure which is which. It's a complex paradigm where things move in ways you can't always predict. But, you *can* do it. With your creativity, you direct your love. And in time, you align your consciousness with the will of the Universe.

Eternity isn't just a concept about the unknown future. You could say it's your schedule. Your job is to create circumstances that challenge love. The opportunities are endless but being human has limits. So it's not so hard to make sense of life even when it's hard to accept. You understand personality types. You understand responsibilities. You understand success and failure. It gives you a way to build support you can trust. The hard thing to understand is that your success is in your values. Physical results don't matter in eternity. Only the love you create is eternal. Your duty is to question love's fairness and find a balance that stands the test of time.

212

Time Well-Lived

What are you supposed to do with all that time? You can make a case for millenniums, but eternity, never-ending time, do you really need that much? I guess it's God's nature. You can make judgments about what's logical but there's a lot hidden about your soul. You accept your soul's love. You accept the need for challenges to make that love grow. You have a sense of life and know that every human being has dealt with these same problems since time began. That's the thing about life. The problems *never* change. From ancient Assyria to modern America, personal and social issues are the same. Every generation has to learn them as if they were new. God knows this. You don't need new problems. You just make new people. They connect as the generations blend, growing through their stages, learning from the ones ahead and teaching those that follow. Then there's the media, even if it's written on clay tablets and parchment, the magic of recorded history endures to instruct new generations with ancient lessons still current today.

How do you create something that lasts forever? You put your love in it. Nothing permanent exists without love. You create that love. You may feel you give too much and get too little. That's what eternity's for. It gives you time to even things out. You grow into your perfection. It sounds odd that the perfection in your soul has to achieve perfection, but that's how you create more love. You create it through fairness. Giving to a charity is about fairness. You have enough while someone else is in need. So you give of yourself to equal things out. You ask yourself about fairness a thousand times a day. Often it's just common sense. Other times it resolves itself over time through deep introspection to develop an honest picture of what's fair when the values are so different. You have to love yourself, not gorge yourself because you fear life will leave you empty. Love's compass will always align fairness with eternity.

You'll wake up tomorrow to a brand new day.

What can you do today that would benefit you forever? You're definitely in the game. You're here so you play. The answer to why you exist; God knows. You exist and you have an idea of your

213

purpose as life interacts with your choices. You have explanations in God's wisdom given over millennia to help you ask the right questions.

The existence of ancient wisdom is God's gift to you. Interpret it as you wish, but thank God for it. I couldn't imagine a more confusing existence than to be without God's guidance. It helps you make better choices and accept your problems as passing conditions. You weren't forced into life. You waited in line. Now it's your turn.

It's not your turn to suffer. It's your turn to meet your challenges. It doesn't seem that way, but you're here for the ride of your life. If you're blessed with a positive sense of yourself, life's a great adventure. But if you've been short-changed, which is the case for most of us, then that's your first job; to achieve an honest sense of who you are and what you want. Then you use self-love to develop a positive attitude. When you know who you are and how life works you can be happy no matter what your situation. You'll feel confident and purposeful. You'll accept your life. You'll feel the pain and disappointment, but it'll pass because you understand that with a positive attitude your problems have value. You'll use your experience. You'll solve your problems. Best of all, you'll learn that you decide your moods so you can feel good whenever you want. At least you'll find the comfort that comes with a positive attitude.

Measuring it doesn't affect eternity. Minutes and hours only give perspective to your progress. You engage life moment to moment with every thought you have. Your life isn't happening tomorrow. Your life is happening now. Your thoughts and feelings are happening now. The love you create, you create in the moment. Results prove themselves when they happen, but you already created the image that inspired them. The pleasure you feel in your hopes is happening now. The dread you feel of the future is happening now. Eternity is the attitude that everything affects who you are. That's happening *now*. You're always thinking about your happiness, whether you have it or not.

Success & Compromise

Success is a compromise of what you want and what you think it's worth to you. First, you negotiate with yourself. It could be anything. You like the car, but what would you pay for it? What if someone else buys it first? You trade values according to your priorities. Compromise determines an equal value of what you get for what you give. You have to feel it's fair. Compromise isn't weakness. Compromise balances your values. Your creative nature isn't limited by what you see. Compromise is only limited by your vision of what else might work. Maybe you don't need that car. You could take the train. That's the best part. Compromise feeds your strongest suit, your creativity.

Compromises are the values that satisfy you. Even when others don't see it, you know the truth of what something's worth to you. There's comfort in the truth because truth and love are eternal. Eternity is a comfortable bed because there's no schedule for your success. Success in eternity includes everything. It's not a pot of gold at the end of the rainbow. It's your thoughts throughout your life, the road that passes through eternity. Your compromises have consequences beyond their results because, again, eternity will always ask you, "Where was love in your decision?"

"Life isn't a destination. It's a journey." That's the saying and it's fine if you can pay for it. The high cost of living means making money matters. Staying alive is your first destination. So how does your imperative to create love correspond with your need to survive? Your success is in bringing these elements together, the temporal and eternal. It's not easy but you're not expected to be an expert. You're supposed to be confronted. You're supposed to find loving solutions to your problems. Your success is in your sincerity, not in your accomplishments. Sincerity is your journey. It's easy to say and hard to trust. You're doing the best you can. That's all that's asked of you. That's why you're alive.

Is it worth the struggle?

Life is hard and seems to go on forever. Your daily experience is a taste of eternity. It's work taking care of yourself. You do well or you suffer, and you don't want to suffer. You want to feel good. Money helps but love is your guarantee. It's like when a cast-off kitten is adopted by a loving family and its life is filled with the joy of belonging. You can feel that joy. Love teaches you faith, hope, and charity. You don't give it much thought, not when you compare it to the time you spend thinking about money. You're so busy living. You rely on love subconsciously. You do something for a friend, think kindly of someone who's passed away, or feel for a stranger's pain. You enjoy your consciousness as you gaze at the sunset releasing your fears. You can feel the goodness in love...and the comfort in eternity.

It's worth it. You feel the love you create. In your forgiveness and compassion, in your hope and faith, you create love. Life is distracting. It's easy to lose your way. Like a fun house full of mirrors, life is designed to fool you. It takes you away from your spiritual nature so you have to find your way back. That's your conflict. Love is eternal but it's easy to think it's unnecessary. Your hungers are immediate. They demand your attention even when they're not important. You have to train your desires to trust you. Willpower isn't enough. Free will is the opportunistic part of your consciousness. You want your senses to trust love. Love is the guiding force in everything. Your soul doesn't direct it. Your soul creates it. God directs it. Know love and you'll know where you're going.

Your journey is to find out where your love and accomplishments meet. Everything counts. A wonderful accomplishment may be insufficient to equalize a life of bad choices. And horrible actions don't negate the love and kindness you created. Love ties everything together. It's your salvation. Human beings have their priorities. God has its priorities. Who's to judge?

Eternally Yours

Eternity is happening in front of you, behind you, and around you. It's the continuity of your experience expanded in all directions. You explored eternity before you came here, and you'll keep exploring eternity as you pass through life to wherever you're going. It's your existence beyond the measure of time. It's your changing consciousness as you move from one lifetime to the next. It's your soul secure in God's love. Eternity, for all its endlessness, is marked by the changes to your consciousness. Changes aren't made over time. Changes are made in the moment. In that moment you have the power to choose one thing over another and create your values.

Eternity is measured by your choices. You create a plan in Spirit and your life reacts to it. You can do anything you want when you trust love's guidance. You can also see what happens when you ignore love's guidance. Eternity isn't the imagined power of immortality, that nothing can ever hurt you. Alive or in Spirit, you still have responsibilities to love. It takes constant effort to keep your consciousness balanced with love. That's what eternity's for. Your accomplishments are important but the time to achieve them doesn't matter. That doesn't mean you'll need till the end of time to get what you want. You'll accomplish many things and start new things again and again. When you're dealing with eternity there's always plenty to do.

You can move forward even while the world stays the same. You know life's processes don't change. From its atomic basics to its endless biology, the world maintains its functions in reliable sciences you can question. It simplifies things so you can do what you do best...be creative. Your responsibility is to give your creativity free rein to wonder about life's possibilities if only things were a bit different. At least, you have the right. It could be as simple as using a push-button to start your car instead of a key or as complicated as forming a new government from factions who were killing each other a few months ago. It's nature and it's people. It's how you're willing to align your dreams with God's plan.

Does anything matter?

Everything matters. For eternity, your time here isn't even a breath. Maybe a hundred lifetimes here isn't even a breath. You give things importance beyond their value because it's your nature to protect yourself. Your soul values your life by just one thing, the love you create. Time has no meaning. Love defines eternity. Not that it's endless but that nothing means anything without love. Love gives each moment its meaning. Eternity doesn't have to be productive. It's not a machine. It's a space filled with love. It expands when there's more love to fill it. As long as there are opportunities to create love, eternity matters.

Your soul knows why you're alive. Listen to it. Have a clear purpose. Appreciate your values. It usually takes an extreme situation to consider your soul's role in life. In peace and desperation are when your soul reveals itself. In the quiet of a chapel or the stress of imminent danger are when your soul makes itself known. Both moods necessitate that you free your mind of unrelated concerns. It's when you *need* to know your soul that you're most sensitive to your spirituality. You stop being a robot lost in social trends. You think for yourself and ask how God can support you.

Love works.

In a world of harsh realities something makes you want to live through it. Even the worst situation has the spark of happiness that could bring you back to life. You know that if a problem is fixed you'll find your happiness again. Life requires a steady hand without adding doubts that could feed your suffering. You learn that most things never become the disaster you imagine. Your concerns demand attention but uncontrolled emotions can easily blow things out of proportion. Problems concern something that's missing. They ask you to think creatively to find a solution. Life asks you to be brave. Love supports your courage as a guarantee. It guarantees your soul with eternity's experience. You don't learn that from books. You learn that by living it.

As grievous as it is, dying solves the most hopeless problem. "They're in a better place now." you say. "They're not suffering anymore." It's not what you want, though some would choose it over suffering years with no hope of recovery. Yet people still want to live. Your soul wants you to experience as much love as you can till your very last breath. Everyone, no matter what their condition, still wants happiness. You wonder why all the pain is necessary, if there isn't an easier way. As long as you have life, there's hope love will find a way to give you happiness. So God tests you to prove it. God wants you to trust it. Love is easy to trust when there's nothing to lose. But would you trust it when you know you're leaving loved ones behind? Love will seek every opportunity to express itself. Your purpose and God's purpose are the same, to create more love by sharing it.

Chapter 10
This is love.

Someone once asked me, "What is love?" I gave them an honest and accurate answer but thinking about it later it felt incomplete. People see things differently and the way they understand things, while similar, is personal. I want you to have the best answer possible on this rarely defined concept that you live with as the foundation for your life. This is what it means to be a loving human being.

1) 1 Corinthians 13. In the Bible, this is an excellent place to start your questions on love. I've never seen anything like it anywhere else. It's the perfect place to see what love means to you as a human being. Different Bibles have different interpretations. They're all good and great to compare. If you want to understand love, read this first.

2) You can feel it. Whether it's love for your family or love for an ideal, it's touchable. It's something physical you can explore. Maybe it needs better definition in human terms, but it's there for you to question.

3) It's about caring. Everything is important because it's all part of Creation. It's your respect for everything.

4) It's the glue of the Universe, the energy that connects everything in a common purpose. It's the power that unifies what had been individualized through Creation. It's the

221

oneness that maintains its wholeness no matter how many pieces it becomes. It's the consciousness in everything. It's your common sense.

5) Love is God. God is everywhere in everything so love is everywhere in everything. You touch God in everything you do. Your love is as practical as any other part of your life. You can communicate with God whenever you like; in your thoughts, feelings, actions, desires, but most of all...in your sincerity. You open yourself to God's essence through love.

6) Love is your spirituality. Your spirituality becomes physical through love. This is God's blessing. It's yours and no one can take it from you. This is where religions help. All religions are the same. They each try to define love and the meaning of right behavior. They're all good from their own perspective so they should each be respected as windows on love.

7) Love connects you to God's healing miracles. Love guarantees you wisdom. Love is your unity with Creation's perfection.

8) You must use love to trust it. The world is a reasonable place. You need proof to support your faith. Try it and see how love guides your life.

9) Faith is trust in love. Hope is the belief love will get you what you want. Charity is the belief there's value in love. And loving God is trust in life.

10) Love is the measure of your life. It's the love you create; the love you give and the love you receive. *This is it!*

Love is yours to explore and enjoy. It's the foundation for everything. Put love first and it'll bless you with success no matter what the outcome.